Cambridge Studies in French

THE DEATH OF
STÉPHANE MALLARMÉ

Cambridge Studies in French
General Editor: MALCOLM BOWIE

Also in the series:

J. M. COCKING
Proust. Collected Essays on the Writer and his Art

THE DEATH OF STÉPHANE MALLARMÉ

Leo Bersani

CAMBRIDGE UNIVERSITY PRESS

CAMBRIDGE

LONDON   NEW YORK   NEW ROCHELLE

MELBOURNE   SYDNEY

Published by the Press Syndicate of the University of Cambridge
The Pitt Building, Trumpington Street, Cambridge CB2 1RP
32 East 57th Street, New York, NY 10022, USA
296 Beaconsfield Parade, Middle Park, Melbourne 3206, Australia

First published 1982

Printed in Great Britain at the University Press, Cambridge

Library of Congress Catalogue Number: 81-3907

British Library Cataloguing in Publication Data
Bersani, Leo
The death of Stéphane Mallarmé. – (Cambridge
studies in French)
1. Mallarmé, Stéphane – Criticism and
interpretation
I. Title
841′.8   PQ2344.Z/
ISBN 0 521 23863 3

CONTENTS

GENERAL PREFACE TO THE SERIES

This new series aims to provide a forum for the discussion of major critical or scholarly topics within the field of French studies. Its distinguishing characteristics are the degree of freedom granted to contributing authors, and the range of subjects covered. Rather than promoting a particular area of academic specialization or any single theoretical approach, authors are invited to address themselves to *problems*, and to argue their solutions in whatever terms seem best able to produce an incisive and cogent account of the matter in hand. The search for such terms will sometimes involve the crossing of boundaries between familiar academic disciplines, or the calling of those boundaries into dispute. Most of the studies will be written especially for the series, though from time to time it will also provide new editions of outstanding works which were previously out of print, or originally published in languages other than English or French.

FOREWORD

As an introduction to his massive work on Mallarmé, Jean-Pierre Richard wrote in 1961: 'Few authors have been more minutely and, on the whole, more successfully studied . . . .'[1] The risk of writing on Mallarmé has, thanks to the impressive amounts of critical intelligence lavished on his work, been somewhat reduced. And yet, however grateful we may feel to all the hard-working *mallarmistes* who have preceded us, we should perhaps also be stunned, even shocked, by the very analyses from which we cannot help but profit. The history of Mallarmé criticism – at least until quite recently – has been that of an amazingly successful de-radicalizing of the Mallarméan text. But it is of course also true that criticism in general – again, at least until quite recently – has always tended to domesticate literature. Criticism has operated on the assumption of a certain opaqueness intrinsic to art; by telling us what art 'is about' (what its subject is, and what it is up to), critical interpretation penetrates and illuminates texts which it thereby rescues from their own enigmatic density.

The Mallarmé criticism to which Richard refers is an exemplary – I would even say parodistic – version of this tendency in all critical activity. For several decades, a group of unreproachably intelligent and resourceful readers from several countries performed an annihilating elucidation of Mallarmé's writing. Specifically, this has meant that the critic of Mallarmé generally substitutes syntactic and narrative coherence for the syntactic and narrative 'puzzles' of a poem or essay by Mallarmé. The Mallarméan text is treated as if it were sick, as if it were *deficient in narrativity*. The assumption has been that Mallarmé's work could be appreciated only if it were first straightened out. Exegesis would be the pre-condition of interpretation – as if exegesis were not in itself a *finalizing* type of interpretive reading. The modest, work-a-day efforts of Mallarmé's countless exegetes were in fact gestures of critical imperialism.

Criticism is perhaps always motivated by the more or less secret project of substituting itself for the texts which it studies; it does away with its objects by embracing them. But if, as I shall be suggesting, such acts of violence, far from being aberrations of criticism, obey unavoidable laws of consciousness itself, exegetical criticism enacts these laws in a repressive rather than in a productive fashion. That is, it simultaneously represses the text *and* the interpretive play which might continue and multiply the text's enigmas in the productively excessive mobility of interpretation itself. Exegetical readings of Mallarmé are, so to speak, vertical replacements of the erased Mallarméan text (they implicitly present themselves as the text's transcendently illuminating reading of itself) rather than a horizontal movement away from the text which leaves the text intact by virtue of the very mode in which it turns away from it....

What are the alternatives to the normalizing of syntax, and the vanquishing of periphrasis by paraphrase, which have characterized exegetical criticism of Mallarmé? The relation between criticism and literature outlined a moment ago has been reversed by a significant part of contemporary criticism. Far from seeking to de-radicalize the literary text, we are now more likely to emphasize the radical unlocatability of meaning in literary language. Criticism has become the place where the radical nature of literature is 'realized' – both articulated and perhaps even, in certain cases, fully enacted. While traditional criticism appeared to set itself the task of making the literary text transparent to understanding, criticism now problematizes its objects by speaking of their sense as multiple, indeterminate, undecidable, mobile, intervallic.... Criticism, far from solving the enigmas of literature, has perhaps even put into question the very category of the enigma by dissolving it in a more radical view of literary language (a view to which narrative resolutions of enigmatic sense are irrelevant) as continuously performing the deferral, or the absence, of its meanings. In a sense, the peculiar achievement of contemporary criticism has been to demonstrate the unreadability of the literary text. The much discussed breakdown of the boundaries between 'critical' and 'literary' writing is partly a function of this demonstration: the critic, unable to read the literary text, can approach his constantly receding object only by (inaccurately) duplicating, in his own writing, its abyssal, receding movements.

My own non-exegetical mobility around, toward, and away from Mallarmé's writing could be considered as a prolegomenon to an essay on sublimation. I have wanted to describe some of the sublimating moves of the Mallarméan text without appealing to the authority of psychoanalytic theory or terminology. I do not use 'sublimation' except in the final pages, and even in that privileged position the word is not meant to provide an interpretive climax or key to all the preceding pages. Rather, I have myself been somewhat surprised to discover that a study of the death of personality and the dismissal of literature's claims to authority – that is, a study of the erasure of (presumed) personal and institutional foundations of successful sublimation – has perhaps also provided a model of what may usefully be called the sublimating process, and more specifically, some preliminary indications of how sublimation differs from both repression and symbolism. A wish to move away, at least temporarily, from my previous work with Freudian texts has therefore resulted – rather predictably and a bit comically – in a circular mobility. But I confess that the pleasure of taking a few speculative risks without the comparative security provided by a psychoanalytic vocabulary prevents me from harshly judging the eventual re-emergence of that vocabulary. Furthermore, the virtue of *not thinking about* sublimation has perhaps been a greater willingness on my part than would otherwise have been the case to recognize the *identity*, in Mallarmé, *between a sexualized mental text and a culturally viable art*. What is truly radical about Mallarmé is perhaps this demonstration that the most refined cultural product need not exercise any repressive authority over human desire.[2]

Nothing is stranger than the textual difficulty which results from this harmonious relation between civilized discourse and desiring impulses. While I of course cannot claim to have protected Mallarmé's seductive unreadability by writing about him, I hope to have suggested that, far from hiding any secret meanings, his difficulty is peculiarly empty – a sign of what I speak of as the restless sociability of desire in his work. Mallarmé's difficulty is the consequence of continuously renewed disappearances – of the author, as well as of the authority of his text. But disappearance in Mallarmé is frequently a procreative act. If his writing makes manifest the negativizing moves of consciousness, it also makes negativity itself an object of irony. No negativizing move of consciousness can cover, and abolish, the differential – and permanently unreadable – moves of an eroticized mental text. Mallarmé's work never stops producing a sense which is nowhere, and this means that Mallarmé is at once impossible to read and extremely easy to read. We should, I think, find him close to the most familiar moves of ordinary consciousness. His writing is really neither hermetic nor exotic; indeed, Mallarmé even re-introduces us to what might be called the energetic domesticity of desiring representations, a domesticity which no amount of exegesis will tame.

1
THE MAN DIES

How does the study of verse lead to the experience of Nothingness?
Toward the end of April 1866, Mallarmé writes to his friend Henri
Cazalis that he has finished a draft of the 'musical opening' of his
poem *Hérodiade*, and that, after three or four more winters of work,
'j'aurai enfin fait ce que je rêve, écrire un Poème digne de Poe et que
les siens ne surpasseront pas.... Malheureusement,' Mallarmé
continues, 'en creusant le vers à ce point, j'ai rencontré deux abîmes,
qui me désespèrent.' One 'abyss' is in Mallarmé's chest: he has
trouble taking deep breaths, and, wondering if he has only a few years
to live, complains of the time lost to art which he must spend teaching
English in order to earn a living. The other 'abyss' is Nothingness,
a 'pensée écrasante' – a crushing or overwhelming thought – which
has made Mallarmé stop working and even lose faith in his poetry.
In this letter, the discovery of Nothingness appears to be correlative
to a sense of the finality of matter:

Oui, *je le sais*, nous ne sommes que de vaines formes de la matière, mais bien
sublimes pour avoir inventé Dieu et notre âme. Si sublimes, mon ami! que
je veux me donner ce spectacle de la matière, ayant conscience d'être et,
cependant, s'élançant forcenément dans le Rêve qu'elle sait n'être pas,
chantant l'Ame et toutes les divines impressions pareilles qui se sont
amassées en nous depuis les premiers âges et proclamant devant le Rien qui
est la vérité, ces glorieux mensonges![1]

What status shall we give to this text? It is a solemn, philosophically
sentimental and yet appealingly juvenile document. Its interest is
somewhat tangential to its apparent message; to a certain extent, it
even lies in a tangentiality in Mallarmé himself. The profound
exploration of verse has the peculiar effect of moving the poet to the
side of his verse. Far from being caught up in his own poetic illusion,
Mallarmé immediately becomes the critic of that illusion. The more
profound his penetration into poetic language, the more acute his
sense of that language's emptiness, of the lack of correspondence

1

between verbal fictions and being. Poetic composition heightens the poet's sense of alienation from poetry; he experiences himself as only a vain form of matter at the very moment he produces the sublime and glorious lies of poetry.

To write *Hérodiade* is therefore a divisive enterprise: it separates Mallarmé's work from Mallarmé's being. And the distance between the two at once becomes the occasion for a further division. We already have matter conscious of being, and plunging into a Dream which it knows is not. Now we have another split, so to speak, in the other direction, and the poet wills into existence a consciousness of the first split as a sublime spectacle. To write poetry is an exercise in ontological analysis: it separates imagination from being, and then produces a consciousness of the process by which the two are separated. To put this in another way, we might say that for Mallarmé the writing of verse is a multiplication of distances; or, in still other terms, poetry generates an ironic consciousness of poetry.

Mallarmé's 'crisis' of the 1860s – the bouts of physical illness, the creative sterility, the metaphysical anguish – is inseparable from his poetic ambitions and experimentation. Without trivializing that crisis, one might note that it is frequently articulated in a context of certain strategic (rather than philosophical) concerns. The passage on the 'two abysses' in the April 1866 letter to Cazalis by no means cancels out Mallarmé's enthusiasm for his recent esthetic achievement. His work on the musical opening of *Hérodiade* is first referred to not as having led to an encounter with Nothingness, but rather as having given rise to an extraordinary self-confidence in Mallarmé. The poem will not be finished for another three or four years, but the poet has already assigned himself an exalted rank in the history of art on the basis of its (as yet unrealized) merits. If the dreams of art are, at best, glorious lies, the historical record of those lies invites both emulation and critical discriminations. An *image d'Épinal* is 'common...compared to a painting by Leonardo da Vinci,' and Mallarmé proudly places himself in the most aristocratic genealogy of art: from the *Mona Lisa* to the *Raven* [sic] to *Hérodiade* (*C*, p. 207).

Mallarmé's meeting with Nothingness takes place in the context of a remarkably well-designed poetic career. On the one hand, his absorbed study of verse paralyzes composition. Almost three years after the letter from which I have quoted, Mallarmé, writing once again to Cazalis, asserts: '...le simple acte d'écrire installe l'hystérie dans ma tête...je ne suis pas encore tout à fait quitte de la crise puisque la dictée à mon bon secrétaire [his wife Marie] et l'impression d'une plume qui marche par ma volonté, même grâce à une autre main, me rend mes palpitations' (*C.*, p. 301). On the other hand, the very terror of writing becomes part of an ambitious literary project. The discovery of Nothingness is followed by the discovery of the Beautiful, and each becomes the subject of a volume in the grand Work outlined in so many of Mallarmé's letters. One version of that outline mentions 'quatre poèmes en prose, sur la conception spirituelle du Néant'; the latter is to provide one section of '"l'ensemble de travaux littéraires qui composent l'existence poétique d'un Rêveur" et qu'on appelle, enfin, son œuvre' (*C.*, pp. 242 and 226).[2] The Work will be the 'image' of the poet's 'spiritual developments' (*C.*, p. 242). The very crisis which threatens the writing of poetry sustains poetic composition. The split between Mallarmé's work and Mallarmé's being is not only a sublime spectacle for the poet; it is also an important subject for his poetic fictions. Poetry is simultaneously the experience and the record of psychic division; it incorporates a fundamentally anti-poetic consciousness of its own emptiness. Mallarmé's paralyzing encounter with Nothingness immediately finds its place in an ambitious program of literary productivity.

To speak of the 1860s only in terms which suggest metaphysical melodrama would therefore be to neglect Mallarmé's constant and extreme attentiveness to the creative advantages of a frequently grave creative sterility. Mallarmé's very existence as a writer is endangered by the solitary years in Tournon and Besançon; at the same time, they are years of apprenticeship in which Mallarmé prepares himself – and others – for his future career as a man of letters. In part, Mallarmé's letters are experimental publicity. They are tentative soundings into the poetic *métier* – ways of sounding like a poet and testing an esthetic. The proposed esthetic will, in large measure, be dropped, and the promised masterwork never delivered; but, as we shall see, the experience of poetry as a kind of separation from the self remains the condition for all the 'inessential' texts which signal both Mallarmé's failure to produce his Work and his entrance into the activity of writing.

The experience of the poet's absence from his verse is precipitated by an artistic credo which equates poetry with a form of subjectivity. Mallarmé begins by defining his work in terms of an impressionistic esthetic. He writes to Cazalis in the fall of 1864 that he has at last begun his *Hérodiade*, 'avec terreur, car j'invente une langue qui doit nécessairement jaillir d'une poétique très nouvelle, que je pourrais définir en ces deux mots: *Peindre, non la chose, mais l'effet qu'elle produit.*' Not content to propose this suppression of the external world in favor of its 'effects,' Mallarmé goes on to suggest that language itself should disappear for the sake of a pure subjectivity: 'le vers ne doit donc pas, là, se composer de mots; mais d'intentions, et toutes les paroles s'effacer devant la sensation' (*C.*, p. 137). A few months later, referring once again to *Hérodiade* in another letter to Cazalis, Mallarmé speaks of having found 'une façon intime et singulière de peindre et de noter des impressions très fugitives,' impressions which follow one another as in a symphony (*C.*, p. 161). And several years later in the essay 'Crise de vers,' Mallarmé appears to reaffirm this subjectivist esthetic when he praises the contemporary poet for having abolished the esthetic 'error' of filling the pages of his book with anything but, for example, 'l'horreur de la forêt, ou le tonnerre muet épars au feuillage; non le bois intrinsèque et dense des arbres.'[3]

Mallarmé's qualified defense of *le vers libre* is based on his interest in the possibility of an unconstrained allusiveness of language to particular impressions. The *vers libre*, freed of the rhythmical constraints of traditional verse, fashions itself according to the 'music' of individual souls ('Toute âme est un nœud rythmique' [*O.C.*, p. 644]). Prose qualifies as poetry, Mallarmé writes in the essay 'Étalages,' when there remains 'quelque secrète poursuite de musique, dans la réserve du Discours' (*O.C.*, p. 375).[4] Within the semantic pursuits of language there are certain rhythmical projects, projects which – at least according to one important current in Mallarmé's thought – displace our attention from the sense of words to those 'cadences' through which wordless impressions simultaneously structure and erase language.

The impressionist esthetic has served as an important guideline in critical readings of Mallarmé. It provides a reasonable explanation for the difficulty of his writing and implicitly proposes a technique by which that difficulty can be reduced (not merely lessened but even abolished). If the poet neglects things for their effects, the critic will infer the former from the latter. The very success with which Mallarmé erases the world of things would presumably authorize the re-establishment of that world by criticism – which is to say that it would authorize a profoundly anti-Mallarméan bias in Mallarmé criticism. Criticism can attempt to verbalize the subjectivity pursued within (or to the side of, or perhaps even against) poetic verbalizations. I will shortly be arguing against this enterprise. We should, however, first of all recognize how logical it is. A psychologically

4

thematic criticism would be the complement to psychologically impressionistic verse. The words of a poem disappear so that we may hear only the cadences of an individual soul; criticism would be the translation of those cadences into language, their *first* adequate verbal expression. The critic reconstitutes the poet's subjectivity by generalizing the impressions or sensations alluded to in his writing into a structure or 'family' of preferred images. Thus, while the pursuit of impressions or sensations by no means implies the wish to portray a coherent personality in literature (Mallarméan impressionism is not designed to construct a self), even a discontinuous subjectivity encourages us to infer a self – that is, a more or less systematic intentionality in which discreet sensations and impressions are grounded. Mallarmé's reader can unify the invisible, nonverbal, fleeting effects of things in stabilized structures of response to the world. Sensations, impressions and intentions form groups, or constellations, which allow the critic to speak of the 'universe' of Mallarmé's subjectivity.

But it is precisely while trying to write verses composed not of words but of impressions that Mallarmé discovers the anguishing distance between his work and his being. Even more: his subjectivist esthetic is promoted during a period when Mallarmé's principal experience appears to be that of his own death. 'Je suis mort,' he writes to Théodore Aubanel in July 1866.[5] And yet in the same paragraph Mallarmé speaks once again of books composed of sensations. What can it mean to transcribe a sensation which no one has had, a sensation without a human subject? It is true that Mallarmé refers in this letter to his resurrection. But 'his' has become immensely problematic: it is not Mallarmé who has come back to life but – to judge from the letters of this period – a kind of structuralizing magnet.'... Tout est si bien ordonné en moi, qu'à mesure, maintenant, qu'une sensation m'arrive, elle se transfigure et va d'elle-même se caser dans tel livre et tel poème. Quand un poème sera mûr, il se détachera' (*C.*, p. 222). The book is first of all internal; Mallarmé, having died, *is* a book in the process of being composed. The written work is merely Mallarmé-as-book having come to fruition, having dropped away – like a fruit from a tree – from a nurturing center. 'Tu vois que j'imite la loi naturelle,' Mallarmé tells Aubanel, and in another letter to the same friend, about two weeks later, Mallarmé claims that he was recently able to outline his entire work after having found the 'key' or 'keystone' or 'center' of his being – 'centre de moi-même, où je me tiens comme une araignée sacrée, sur les principaux fils déjà sortis de mon esprit, et à l'aide desquels je tisserai *aux points de rencontre* de merveilleuses dentelles, que je devine, et qui existent déjà dans le sein de la Beauté' (*C.*, pp. 222, 224–5).[6]

Having died, Mallarmé displaces the authorship of his poems from his defunct self to the universe. Thus, in what is perhaps his best known letter to Cazalis, Mallarmé proclaims: '...je suis maintenant impersonnel et non plus le Stéphane que tu as connu, – mais une aptitude qu'a l'Univers spirituel à se voir et à se développer, à travers ce qui fut moi. Fragile comme est mon apparition terrestre, je ne puis subir que les développements absolument nécessaires pour que l'Univers retrouve, en ce moi, son identité' (*C.*, p. 242).[7] Such orphic pronouncements may be taken as Mallarmé's effort to *think* the eerie experience of literary expression as the abolition of an identifiable human source of literary expression. The attempt to render the effects of things rather than things themselves has, surprisingly, erased the individual subject necessary, one would think, to register such effects. And it is as if impressions and sensations themselves were then projected onto the external world as a kind of ordering, nonmaterial structure of the very objects which produce them. Mallarmé thus proposes a non-psychological version of phenomena – such as intentions, impressions and sensations – which are ordinarily assumed to be constitutive of psychological subjectivity. 'Toute âme est une mélodie,' but Beauty is the music without the individual (*C.*, p. 363).

By what logic has a project of self-expression (the wish to make poetry transparent to the most particular cadences or rhythms of individual responses to the world) led to Mallarmé's death? Self-concentration destabilizes the self. It is as if the very attempt to hold on to a thought or a sensation produced a kind of snapping movement away from that thought or sensation. The project of making verse transparent to the music of individual souls is realized with a certain ontological violence. At times, Mallarmé describes this violence as a decomposition of being. Three days after announcing to Cazalis that he is now impersonal, 'une aptitude qu'a l'Univers spirituel à se voir et à se développer, à travers ce qui fut moi,' Mallarmé writes to Eugène Lefébure that he is 'véritablement décomposé, et dire qu'il faut cela pour avoir une vue très – une de l'Univers! Autrement, on ne sent d'autre unité que celle de sa vie.' Mallarmé must destroy a merely historical or biographical unity in order to become the 'sacred spider' weaving with the threads of his own mind the 'marvelous lacework' of objective Beauty. But he also laments the destructive divisions of his being; the concentrated self seems to be immediately recognized as a partial self. Mallarmé complains to Lefébure of having worked the preceding summer with thoughts coming only from his brain, and he describes an effort he made to stop working only cerebrally: '…j'essayai de ne plus penser de la tête et, par un effort désespéré, je roidis tous mes nerfs (en pectus) de façon à produire une vibration en gardant la pensée à laquelle je travaillais alors, qui devient le sujet de cette vibration, ou une impression – et j'ébauchai tout un poème longtemps rêvé, de cette façon' (*C.*, p. 249).[8] In this curiously abstract analysis of what might be taken as a willful eroticizing of thought, the vibration produced by stiffened nerves 'receives' a purely cerebral thought and transforms it into an impression. Mallarmé is now thinking, as he writes, 'with his entire body'; thought becomes concrete when it provides the occasion or content for (when it is the 'subject' of) a vibrating stiffness of nerves. A 'desperate' (and desperately ingenious) effort at self-concentration is meant to forestall the explosive effects of…self-concentration.

But the vibrating self-concentration which emerges as a major creative mood of Mallarmé's early years does not immobilize the 'thought' which it eroticizes. On the contrary: once a thought begins to vibrate, it also begins to be scattered or disseminated. In his major poetic achievement during the period of the letters to which I have been referring, Mallarmé investigates the possibility of non-disseminating vibrations. *Hérodiade* could be thought of as Mallarmé's attempt to imagine an escape from the consequences of the mode in which the work is composed. Both Mallarmé's heroine and his own poetic procedures move between extreme versions of mobility and immobility. There is a strong pull toward specular immobilizations in *Hérodiade*. This is the period in Mallarmé's career when his interest in musical effects in poetry mainly takes the form of verbal repetitions. Certain words – such as *aurore, ombre, or* – keep returning in the first two sections of *Hérodiade*.[9] They of course designate thematic centers in the poem, but, perhaps more powerfully, they operate like simplifying and stabilizing reflectors. It is as if lexical mirrors had been placed throughout the poem, mirrors which pick up reflections of earlier verses and, to a certain extent, reduce the verbal heterogeneity of the work through the force of a shimmering sameness.

The variety of the poetic space of *Hérodiade* is almost devoured by this pursuit of the verbal couple, by emphatic replications which create a dizzying structural stability. All these repetitions help to organize the sense of the poem, but their principal function appears to be the very placing of the repetition itself. Mallarmé's ingenious rhymes serve the same function even more clearly: a few startling rhyme-couples (such as *lune* and *l'une*, and the negative *pas* with *pas* as step) encourage our receptiveness to various sorts of linguistic pairing. Far from merely punctuating rhythmic units, such rhymes actually divert our attention from rhythm and make us *stop* at a surprising sameness of sound which, so to speak, wins out over the more obvious but now suppressed semantic diversity. Hérodiade's narcissistic ambitions are most satisfactorily realized in Mallarmé's arresting (astonishing and immobilizing) poetic procedures.

The pairing of *l'une* with *lune* is considerably easier to accomplish than the specularization of Hérodiade herself. The princess seeks to find and to fix her own image. The main obstacle to Hérodiade's narcissistic project is that *she cannot be found*; in order to possess her identity, Hérodiade must first of all be sure of her location. The very first question the nurse asks in the 'Scène' is whether she is seeing Hérodiade or 'l'ombre d'une princesse [the shadow of a princess].' Hérodiade is referred to several times in the poem as an 'ombre,' and when she seeks her memories under the frozen water of her mirror's surface, she appears to herself as 'une ombre lointaine [a distant shadow].' The sense of self in *Hérodiade* is inseparable from a sense of both distance and anteriority.

But in order to understand the notion of shadow-being, we should first of all note some apparent contradictions. If Hérodiade is a mere shadow, she is also a star. She speaks, for example, in the 'Scène' of her 'pudeur grelottante d'étoile [shivering star-like modesty],' and she asserts that her mirror 'reflète en son calme dormant/Hérodiade au clair regard de diamant.'[10] What does it mean to be simultaneously darkness and light, a shadow and a bright diamond? Mallarmé, who claimed that he hadn't slept for years, reportedly told L. Dauphin of a month during which his insomnia had been so painful that, in order to work, he had to put his hand in front of his eyes after each sentence he wrote, and keep it there for a long while, in order to breathe in a little darkness.[11] The darkness is necessary not as a relief or rest from work, but in order to make work – writing – possible. Mallarmé's wakefulness is the enemy of his thought. We might say – generalizing the Mallarméan experience – that insomnia impedes the functioning of thought, the suspension (even more: the suppression) of external reality on which thought depends. Thought is a clarifying murder; it illuminates the world by plunging it into darkness. Thus the darkness of night and of sleep is necessary to the light of consciousness. *This light is a night.* And to speak of consciousness as a de-realizing illumination of the world, or as a replicating abolition of its objects, is not even to propose a paradox; no logical category can adequately describe the fundamental operation of mind on which all movements of logic depend.[12]

The illuminations of thought are nocturnal or shadow versions of reality. They repeat reality somewhat as a shadow repeats its object: by simultaneously darkening and defining it. From this perspective, Hérodiade's perception of herself as both shadow and star or diamond becomes intelligible as a vision of the nature of thought. But I should say at once that, at this level of abstraction, the notion of vision itself becomes unintelligible, and in *Hérodiade* Mallarmé brilliantly uses narcissism as a psychological metaphor for the replicating and annihilating operations of thought. The attempt to achieve self-possession through specular self-immobilization is, in the poem, a dramatic figure for the inevitably abortive adherence of thought to its object. In both cases, separation is at once the condition for an effort to fix the self (or to immobilize a thought object, or a thought thought), and the guarantee that such an effort will fail. Hérodiade moves away from herself *by* seeking herself; she is a shadow-self to the extent that she has become the *thought of* herself.

Hérodiade's self-contemplation is, by definition, a kind of self-removal: she has lost herself (existentially, historically, as someone with *souvenirs* and not only *songes*) by virtue of her ontologically divisive interest in herself. 'Je viens de passer une année effrayante,' as Mallarmé confides to Cazalis: 'ma Pensée s'est pensée, et est arrivée à une Conception pure' (*C.*, p. 240).[13] The thinker is lost (appears to die) in the very movement by which he becomes the object of his own attention. Even more radically, once the thinker of his thought has become nothing more than a replicating reflex, thinking can no longer *go on*; and, as Mallarmé writes in the letter just quoted from, he has to look at himself in a mirror 'in order to think' – that is, in order to certify the existence of a thinking subject whose thinking *can* be thought in a reflexive duplication of its own movements.

Now if narcissism illustrates the replicating movement of all thought, it also enacts the tendency of thought to immobilize its object. Thinking the world is at once a removal from, and an attempted replication of the world; but this replication includes the project of resuscitating the abolished world in the form of stabilized ideas or concepts. Thought seeks to be arrested by solidified sense, to extract and to possess the 'meanings' of its own movements. Narcissism exacerbates and explodes this project of consciousness.

The solidified sense pursued in narcissism is not conceptual but corporeal: evidence of a self is provided by the image of a body in a mirror. The self, however, may be nothing more than a derivation of mental mechanics, the compensatory sign of thought's exhaustion with its own objectless replications, with the ceaseless erasures of its own representations. Hérodiade, the bright shadow of a princess, wanders through her palace grounds, and stops in front of her mirror in search of her errant self. Her continuous movement away from herself is thus (uselessly) contravened by an attempt to catch a self prior to that movement. Going away is misinterpreted as going towards, and a nostalgia for psychic origins leads to a positing of goals and climaxes to psychic mobility. The movements of consciousness are always productively mistaken replications of its objects; the narcissistic consciousness would substitute for these non-mimetic replications a perfect identity between thought and its objects. But only the illusory being reflected in a mirror realizes that identity. The mirror deceives human consciousness into believing that it can be externalized as pure representation, that the movements of a desiring being can be immobilized in a total form.

And yet, as I have said, Hérodiade significantly does not find such a form in her mirror. The fragility, and ultimately the failure of the narcissistic project in the poem are indicated by the princess's difficulty in producing a reflection of herself, as well as by her fright at what she sees. Either she finds an exact but curiously distant replica of herself, or she sees the 'nudity' of her 'scattered dream.' The first image is nothing more than the repetition of the shadow which dreams of discovering a mineral-like hardness and luster in the mirror; and the second image – if it can be called that – is perhaps a frightening (and unimaginable) 'representation' not of a lustrous, stellar self but of the very abstractness by which that dream separates itself from the shadowy movements of consciousness. *Hérodiade* is a poem of distress: distress at the failure of the narcissistic dream, and especially at the consequences of not being able to immobilize consciousness. The anecdotal sign of narcissism's defeat is Hérodiade's confession, after the nurse's departure, that the 'naked flower' of her lips has been lying, and that she is waiting for an 'unknown thing,' an event which may simply be the 'thawing' of her adolescent, mineral-like hardness and her consenting initiation into sexuality. But this initiation would merely be one result of the more fundamental failure of a dream of self-possession, a failure which is itself the corollary of certain unavoidable movements of consciousness.

Perhaps the best way to describe these movements is to consider their intrusion into what I have called the work's specularizing procedures. On the one hand, there are all the verbal and structural repetitions which tend to create a kind of monumental stillness in the poem. A system of verbal reflectors throughout the piece works toward the abolishing of intervallic differences. On the other hand, there is an extraordinary amount of what might be called unstable designation in *Hérodiade*. The poem's difficulty is largely due to the sliding identities of persons and things, to casual and unexplained shifts in the register of being. This is particularly true of the 'Ouverture ancienne.'[14] I am thinking, for example, of the metamorphoses of *plis*: from the 'useless folds' of the tapestry in Hérodiade's room in stanza two to the 'yellow folds of thought' in which the voice of the next stanza 'drags,' to the 'stiffened folds' of the shroud-consciousness evoked by the nurse, and finally to the dream-book folds no longer inscribed on the unwrinkled linen of Hérodiade's unused bed. Or, in the second stanza, there is the curious displacement of one of the sibyls. They are first mentioned as figures woven into the tapestry in Hérodiade's room, but then one of them is described as being part of the design on the nurse's dress in the closed ivory chest. Even more: we could think of this same movable sibyl as not only displaced but also metamorphosed: she 'seems' to be an 'aroma,' which in turn may come from a sachet perhaps in the chest or may be the odor of the wilted flowers near Hérodiade's bed. Hérodiade's room, which the beginning of the stanza encourages us to visualize as a fixed tableau seen through the window's frame from the courtyard below, is actually a scene of fantastic movements: the gesture of the sibyls offering their aged fingernails to the Magi ('offrant leur ongle vieil aux Mages') on the tapestry, the 'flight' of the sibyl-aroma, the prowling of the scent of cold bones ('un arôme d'os froids rôdant sur le sachet'),[15] and the ambiguous movement – of an aroma carrying an aroma of cold bones, *or* of an aroma of cold bones bearing the scent of a 'touffe de fleurs' – between the ivory chest and Hérodiade's bed (a movement whose point of departure may be either the chest or the bed, or both at once, or neither one).

This is an awkward summary of a few passages of the 'Ouverture ancienne,' but I think that the poem itself is an awkward mixture of immobilizing strategies and what appears to be the distressing mobility of its images. The balancing factors are excessively obvious, and the unexplained displacements and metamorphoses block the poem's narrative progression. This ambitious work may thus strike us as esthetically pretentious; it is dramatically thin, and yet its structure and texture are over-worked, and over-wrought. Excessively ingenious rhymes, excessively neat structural repetitions, excessively daring narrative discontinuities: it is not too hard to sympathize with Albert Thibaudet's dismissive description of *Hérodiade* as a cold masterpiece of technical virtuosity, a 'morceau de concours.'[16] But even if the poem strikes us as a brilliant 'exercise,' as Mallarmé's most 'literary,' even academic work, its over-wrought quality is perhaps the effect of an extremely dramatic play of conflicting pressures in the poem, pressures which will never entirely disappear from Mallarmé's writing.

The sliding identities which I mentioned a moment ago subvert the specular recognitions to which Hérodiade aspires *and* the impressionistic esthetic which presumably governs the composition of Mallarmé's poem. I have spoken of lexical mirrors scattered throughout the work; but, as the metamorphoses of the word *plis* suggest, repetition is not only a structurally immobilizing factor but also works to de-stabilize sense. An echo turns out to be also a displacement. The 'yellow folds of thought' and the 'stiffened folds' of the shroud do not merely send us back to the folds of tapestry in the preceding stanza. They initiate differences, differences all the more disorienting in that the word 'folds' applied to a shroud repeats (unlike the folds of thought) the literal plausibility of folds in a tapestry, at the same time that the shroud itself is a startling metaphor for the vanquished and exhausted consciousness from which the memory-filled voice evoked in stanza 3 painfully rises. A certain narrative logic (according to which the various uses of *plis* both characterize the nurse and provide an apt metaphor for the inert burden of consciousness) is disrupted by the rhetorical wandering of the word *plis*: from its merely denoting the tapestry's visible folds to a metaphorical status in 'les plis jaunes de la pensée,' and finally back to a denotative function within the elaborate metaphor of the shroud. The specular effects and stabilizing power of recurrence are thus qualified by *a*-symmetrical repetitions in *Hérodiade*. In the case of *plis*, there is even something lopsided in the symmetry itself. Sound repetition is almost emphatically divorced from semantic repetition: the reflections of sense which metaphorically describe thought for us in a coherent way are really provided by the adjectives ('useless,' 'yellow,' and 'old' and 'stiffened'), and the sense is one to which the word *plis* itself rather feebly contributes, to which it merely *lends itself*.

The very beginning of the 'Ouverture ancienne' provides us with a condensed version of both the specular and the anti-specular or *a*-symmetrical pressures in *Hérodiade*. Here are the first seven verses of the poem:

> Abolie, et son aile affreuse dans les larmes
> Du bassin, aboli, qui mire les alarmes,
> Des ors nus fustigeant l'espace cramoisi,
> Une Aurore a, plumage héraldique, choisi
> Notre tour cinéraire et sacrificatrice,
> Lourde tombe qu'a fuie un bel oiseau, caprice
> Solitaire d'aurore au vain plumage noir....[17]

The claustrophobic effects of what I have been calling Mallarmé's specularizing intentions are immediately evident here. The passage is extravagantly self-reflexive. The sound *a* is repeated 17 times, seven times in the first two verses. *Aboli* in verse 2 sends us back (with the slight asymmetry of a masculine rather than a feminine ending) to the initial, and initiating *abolie*, just as *plumage* in verse 7 reflects *plumage* in verse 4, and the *aurore* of verse 7 repeats (again, in slightly a-symmetrical fashion: the capital A is dropped) the *Aurore* of verse 4. Such repetitions of words and letters, as well as all the internal rhymes, practically bring the poem to a standstill; the first seven verses of *Hérodiade* are almost an immobile verbal block, a mass in which the only movement is one of shimmering internal reflections. The monotony of sameness immediately plunges us into the desolate atmosphere which the nurse will continue to describe. Here, one might argue, is an excellent example of what it means to describe 'not the object itself, but the effect which it produces.' Impressions of sinister stillness, and of potentially violent negations, are communicated before any attempt is made to establish narrative coherence. Dawn, for example, is identified three verses after the nurse's *sense of* the dawn (as 'abolished,' as plunging its 'frightful wing' into the pool) is given.

But the opening passage of *Hérodiade* undermines the very symmetries which it so carefully establishes. Repetition is accompanied by ontological dislocation. The identity of bird-dawn is no sooner confirmed than the vehicle of that metaphor is repeated as, apparently, a real bird that has fled the tower. However, the words 'caprice/Solitaire d'aurore au vain plumage noir' can be read in several ways. They could refer to the bird's flight (it was a solitary caprice which took place at dawn, a caprice having, strangely, a 'vain plumage noir'), or they might be in apposition to 'oiseau,' in which case 'vain plumage noir' becomes more plausible while caprice as a synonym for bird obviously becomes less plausible. But we might of course also connect the expression to the Dawn's choice of 'notre tour cinéraire et sacrificatrice': that choice is the caprice of a dawn already referred to, in verse 4, as having a 'plumage héraldique' (now modified as 'vain' and 'noir.') 'Aurore' in 'caprice solitaire d'aurore' can thus either refer to the subject of the action (dawn's choice of the tower) or merely have an adverbial status (it tells us when the bird's flight took place). Furthermore, we shortly discover that the beautiful bird is also Hérodiade, who has left her rooms and is walking through the palace grounds. Consequently, the first four verses may express the nurse's sense of the princess's having abandoned her rooms. Dawn has entombed itself, has been 'abolished,' in the equally abolished pool; birds and swans no longer inhabit 'l'eau morne'; and the princess's room has been abandoned by Hérodiade, to whom 'le cygne/inoubliable,' of verses 10 and 11 may refer.[18]

The similarities among these instances are clear, and yet the passage which exploits their similarities is extremely obscure. If the reader is disoriented by Mallarmé's writing in *Hérodiade*, it is not because the poem has an exceptional metaphorical complexity, but rather because Mallarmé gives us ontological sliding rather than metaphorical resemblances. That is, what interests him is not that Hérodiade is *like* a bird or a swan, but rather that, *in being Hérodiade, she is also a swan.* Somewhat like the movable sibyl who also seems to be an aroma, the princess is not fundamentally more Hérodiade, so to speak, than 'she' is the dawn or a bird in flight (or a bird with a 'frightful wing').

The kind of shifting that may occur in a metaphorical relationship does not usually affect the priority accorded to one of the terms. Even Proust, who might appear to be destroying this priority when he claims, in *Le Temps retrouvé*, that the interest of a metaphorical joining together of two distinct objects or sensations lies in the emergence of an immaterial, timeless 'essence' common to those objects or sensations, always distinguishes between the literal term and the figurative term. Metaphorical terms are, it is true, interchangeable in *A la Recherche du temps perdu*, and the density of the novel's texture is due less to its range of reference than to the multiple functions served by a privileged set of references. At Doncières, to take just one example, images drawn from art elucidate military strategy; later on in the work, jealousy will be described partly in terms drawn from the military life. In both cases, what might be called an essence of the Manoeuver disengages itself from the juxtaposed terms of painting, military campaigns and the tactics inspired by jealousy.

But in neither case does a supra-temporal essence disperse the narrative ordering of terms. The actual episode – life in a garrison or life in a Paris apartment with Albertine – is never lost from sight; it is the ground, or the focus, of every description. As a result, the other term of each extended metaphor simultaneously de-temporalizes the narrative and reinforces narrative sequence and coherence. Even in a lyrical poem as exclusively metaphorical as Shakespeare's Sonnet 73 (*That time of year...*), the images of autumn, twilight, and a dying fire occupy almost the entire piece, and yet we are of course meant to see them as vehicles for the implicit tenor of age. If, as Proust claims, metaphors disengage a supra-temporal essence, they work toward the elimination or at least the insignificance of differences in the world by emphasizing a community of sameness. And to the extent that they maintain differences within the compared qualities themselves, these distinctions are hierarchical in that one term has an historical or perceptual priority over another 'imaginary' term evoked in order to elucidate a 'real' or concretely experiential point of departure.

In *Hérodiade*, on the other hand, the appearance of a strong narrative priority is undermined by the fact that description blocks rather than facilitates narrative progress. Hérodiade is not more satisfactorily described as a result of the various images which appear to refer to her: rather, it is as if the poet's thinking of Hérodiade were problematized by all the *other* thoughts which characterize – precisely, and paradoxically – his thought *of her*. The extraordinarily easy movements in the poem – movements which operate against all the immobilizing factors – are metamorphic rather than metaphoric. The *addition* of identities in *Hérodiade* works against the reduction of all identities to a specular sameness (in which the dawn and the swans would merely reflect the princess.) The abolished dawn inaccurately replicates the absent princess; toward the end of the 'Ouverture,' Hérodiade, 'exilée en son cœur précieux [exiled in her precious heart],' is a way of thinking 'un cygne cachant en sa plume ses yeux [a swan hiding its eyes in its plumage];' and the sibyl on the nurse's bleached dress is at once a misplaced tapestry pattern and an aroma from another part of the room.

As these examples suggest, the poem is less successful in proposing likenesses than in recording a sameness among different mental images. The latter is a more fundamental operation of consciousness than the metaphoric process. To metaphorize objects of consciousness is already to be concerned about the legitimacy of transporting one object to another, of rearranging objects in our perceptual and imaginary space. *Hérodiade* gives us something more primitive: a relation legitimized by nothing more than the fact that one term manifests the activity of thinking the other term. Difference is merely a function of the snapping away of consciousness from its object; and identity can be equivalent to absolute difference (sibyl = aroma) because it consists of a replicating movement rather than of perceived resemblances.

I said at the beginning of this discussion of *Hérodiade* that the principal obstacle to self-possession in the poem is the unlocatability of the self. The nurse and the princess are fascinated by infinitely remote or unlocatable realities. In the first stanza, the nurse speaks of the swan (and perhaps, obliquely, also of Hérodiade) plunging into the 'pale mausoleum' of its feathers a head 'désolée/Par le diamant pur de quelque étoile, mais/Antérieure, qui ne scintilla jamais.' I am thinking also of the voice buried under the folds of the shroud of consciousness, as well as of those 'ors ignorés,' invoked by Hérodiade, 'gardant leur antique lumière/Sous le sombre sommeil d'une terre première,'[19] and, finally, of the princess's 'distant shadow' which appears to her in the 'deep hole' of her mirror. Anecdotally, all these haunting distances remain somewhat enigmatic in the poem; they become more intelligible as figures for the peculiar remoteness of Hérodiade as an object of description for Mallarmé himself. The nostalgic mood of the princess's narcissism is perhaps best explained by the system of ambiguous designation in the poem, by what may have been the poet's own agonized discovery that to fix an impression is to lose its source, to disperse the person whom impressions are supposed to designate and to characterize.

The death of self announced in Mallarmé's letters can be thought of as the consequence of the poet's subjectivist esthetic. The transformation of thought into impressions – a transformation produced by taut, vibrating nerves – is a function of mobility. To put this in other terms, the eroticizing of thought destroys the thinking subject as a stable identity. Mallarmé wished to fix impressions, but the result of his self-concentration appears to have been an acceleration of the moving away which I have spoken of as intrinsic to all thought. What Mallarmé called thinking with his body can also be formulated as a masturbatory attention to certain images,[20] an attention which, inevitably, cannot stop producing other images in its annihilating replication of mental objects of *jouissance*. Sexual fantasy is thinking with an especially liberal margin of error and *errance*. The compositional procedures of *Hérodiade* record the moves of a sexualized mental text. Mallarmé's specularizing strategies are attempts to reduce, even to abolish all the inexplicable, anguishing distances created by excited thought, just as Hérodiade's narcissism is the princess's wished-for solution to the unending self-remoteness which is the price of her secret wish to be shattered by the desiring look of another.

Perhaps the most important lesson to be drawn from all this is the *sheer exteriority of subjectivity*. The description of the mind is a description of dawn and of swans and of stagnant pools; or of yellow folds, or 'un confus amas d'ostensoirs refroidis [a heap of monstrances gone cold],' or the pure lacework of a finely stitched shroud. The attempt to hold on to an impression multiplies images of the world. What Mallarmé referred to as his own death was perhaps his experience of wandering among alien images evoked by his intense concentration on his own sensations, impressions and intentions.

But this last word raises a crucial question: to what extent do all those images express intentionality, outline a unique set of projects toward the world? If subjectivity is exteriority, the latter may nonetheless chart an interiority no less real *and* analyzable for taking the form of a certain picture of the world. If introspection leads to abolished pools, tomblike towers, yellow folds, and incensed stars rather than to sentiments and faculties, there is perhaps no reason to abandon the notion of personality along with the psychologically analytic vocabulary which has usually been used to describe personality. Can the techniques of analysis change without our questioning the most fundamental assumptions about the object of analysis?

Mallarmé appears to provide the most conservative answer to this question. Nothing is easier than to find a family of images in his work which conveniently present themselves as alternatives to dominant feelings or passions, alternatives which alter the atmosphere of psychology without putting its validity into question. One can reasonably claim that Mallarmé's poems of the 1860s establish a comparatively small family of images which will characterize his work until his death, and that on the basis of this familial network one can discover that universe of the imagination which Jean-Pierre Richard has so magisterially delineated in *L'Univers imaginaire de Mallarmé*. From the very beginning, there is a recognizable thematic structure in the poet's work. With elegance and thoroughness, Richard tracks down the recurrences of preferred images: windows, transparent lakes and windows, the blue sky, swans, folds, fountains, winter, wings and feathers, blood-red sunsets, the foam of waves, shipwrecks. But to make such a heterogeneous list of images is to miss the coherence of Mallarmé's 'imaginary universe.' Richard's study leaves no doubt about the phenomenological unity which sustains the recurrent images of Mallarmé's work. Furthermore, this unity does not merely characterize one period of Mallarmé's life. Certain images are naturally more dominant in some pieces than in others, and these differences indicate affective variations both from one poem to another and from one time to another, but none of this should affect our confidence in the translatability of Mallarmé's thematic imagery into a phenomenological portrait of the Mallarméan imagination.

And yet Mallarmé the person is dead – *as a result of* wandering in precisely that world which provides the thematic critic with the material for his portrait of a unified and coherent human subjectivity. How can this be? Richard thematizes Mallarmé's work as an effort to solve 'a problem of upward dynamic movement: in a world whose laws are dispersion and entropy, where can the initial impulse towards an ascending movement be found?'[21] This is subtle and, in a sense, right. But it is also a critical version of those immobilizing strategies by which Hérodiade seeks to possess her own image, as well as of those equally immobilizing strategies by which Mallarmé seeks to control intervals which would otherwise function as radically differentiating spaces within his poem. Richard allows for temporal movement and change within the system of Mallarméan imagery, but the movement which he ignores is precisely that replicating-abolishing movement which has no other intention than to repeat a phenomenon of excited consciousness. And that mobility makes for ontological discontinuity among thematically related images. The latter should perhaps be thought of as one of the super-structures of consciousness. Far from expressing that immediate contact with the world of what Gaston Bachelard called our material imagination, the system of preferential images investigated by thematic or phenomenological criticism is already a *structuralizing strategy*. It is the result of reflective movements of mind, although the reflection is of course not of the same order – and not at the same level of consciousness – as in, say, a system of philosophical thought.

The type of criticism practised by Bachelard, Richard and Georges Poulet is at once persuasive and repressive. It would be impossible to imagine a more perceptive study of thematic imagery in Mallarmé's work than *L'Univers imaginaire de Mallarmé*, but Richard never looks suspiciously at the very activity (in the poet and in the critic) which creates such networks. The images catalogued by both thematic criticism and most psychoanalytic criticism appear to be obsessive modes of contact with the world; we should also remember that they are highly visible modes of contact. That is, they are obsessive without being secretive; indeed, they are the writer's preferred version of his own intelligibility. A criticism of deep intentionality (whether it be phenomenological or psychoanalytic) invites us to locate such intentionality in specific themes or images; but it neglects (because it shares) the *intention to create intentionality* as a means of disguising the discontinuity between the act of thinking and the object of thought. Thus thematic criticism is in complicity with the repressive activity in the literary work itself by which the moves of consciousness are concealed by a stabilizing intelligibility of consciousness.

It is precisely that intelligibility which Mallarmé will come to treat as negligible. This is not to say that he rids himself of it, or even that he repudiates it: his thematic system – his 'imaginary universe' – is evident from the childhood verse to the *Coup de dés* of 1897. But *Hérodiade* – to re-phrase my main point about that poem – can be read as an ambivalent rejection of the very consistencies which justify and nourish thematic and psychoanalytic criticism. The distressful failure of Hérodiade's narcissistic project is the poetic form taken by Mallarmé's willingness to renounce the specular securities of an historically coherent 'person.' And what he refers to as his death, far from being another theme in his writing, is the move which ruins the possibility of thematic understanding. For it is a continuous moving away from stabilizing (and obsessive) images. Mallarméan death is a state of radically unsettled being, a state in which the poet is always different from whatever may be said about him. What can be said, however, will not be erased; rather, it will remain in order to create the points between which Mallarmé will be, merely, different from them. The themes of a self do not disappear when Mallarmé 'dies,' but they do become psychologically inert; they memorialize the personality to which they posthumously refer.

The difference between Mallarmé as an intelligible historical person and Mallarmé as depersonalizing movements of consciousness can be traced in the two versions of 'Le Pitre châtié.'

Pour ses yeux, – pour nager dans ces lacs, dont les quais
Sont plantés de beaux cils qu'un matin bleu pénètre,
J'ai, Muse, – moi, ton pitre, – enjambé la fenêtre
Et fui notre baraque où fument tes quinquets.

Et d'herbes enivré, j'ai plongé comme un traître
Dans ces lacs défendus, et, quand tu m'appelais,

19

Baigné mes membres nus dans l'onde aux blancs galets,
Oubliant mon habit de pitre au tronc d'un hêtre.

Le soleil du matin séchait mon corps nouveau
Et je sentais fraîchir loin de ta tyrannie
La neige des glaciers dans ma chair assainie,

Ne sachant pas, hélas! quant s'en allait sur l'eau
Le suif de mes cheveux et le fard de ma peau,
Muse, que cette crasse était tout le génie!

(version of 1864)

Yeux, lacs avec ma simple ivresse de renaître
Autre que l'histrion qui du geste évoquais
Comme plume la suie ignoble des quinquets,
J'ai troué dans le mur de toile une fenêtre.

De ma jambe et des bras limpide nageur traître,
A bonds multipliés, reniant le mauvais
Hamlet! c'est comme si dans l'onde j'innovais
Mille sépulcres pour y vierge disparaître.

Hilare or de cymbale à des poings irrité,
Tout à coup le soleil frappe la nudité
Qui pure s'exhala de ma fraîcheur de nacre,

Rance nuit de la peau quand sur moi vous passiez,
Ne sachant pas, ingrat! que c'était tout mon sacre,
Ce fard noyé dans l'eau perfide des glaciers.

(version of 1887)[22]

    If we consider the poem thematically, we may be able to account for the poet's revisions only through a rather conventional distinction between manner and substance. In both versions, Mallarmé appears to be using the image of a clown who jumps through the canvas wall of a circus tent into the lakes, and/or the nets, or a woman's eyes as a dramatic metaphor for the artist who either betrays his Muse for sensual pleasure, or mistakenly believes that he can still be an artist if he renounces the given materials of his craft (the clown's make-up; perhaps the imagery which 'disguises' simple statement, or the inherited language from which individual poems are forged). From this perspective, we might say that Mallarmé does away with the narrative continuities of the first version in order, principally, to bring us closer to the clown's subjectivity – to his sensations and intentions. The poem naturally becomes more obscure, but the gain in dramatic immediacy is considerable. Thus, the perception of the woman's eyes as lakes is no longer spelled out ('Pour ses yeux, – pour nager dans ces lacs'), but is rather given as an unexplained verbal equivalence in the first two words of the poem: 'Yeux, lacs avec ma simple ivresse de renaître.' And, in the most striking example of this apparent effort to make words transparent to sensation, the effect of the sun striking the swimming clown's naked body is rendered in verse 9 by 'Hilare or de cymbale à des poings irrité.' The image is explained in verse 10 ('Tout à coup le soleil frappe la nudité'), whereas the earlier version of the first tercet had been all explanation. The reader's task in the later version consists less in establishing a correct narrative line (which remains comparatively clear) than in translating verbal analogues of sensations back into sensations. 'Hilare or de cymbale' becomes transparent to sensations (of joyously bathing in the 'loud,' reverberating golden sunlight) thanks to a critical exercise which erases language by (verbally...) elucidating the rightness of certain words as a translation of sensations experienced, originally, without language.

There is, however, a way of considering Mallarmé's revisions not as strategies designed to increase the dramatic immediacy of his theme, but rather as a means of changing the status of meaning itself in the poem. To begin with, the first condensation ('Yeux, lacs') makes the love theme problematic; we really have no grounds for asserting that the clown leaps, as he says in the first version, in order to swim in the woman's eyes. Instead of a rather clichéd tension between love and art, the final version asks the simpler, and yet more puzzling, question of whether or not a certain kind of leap is consistent with the 'consecration' of a performing artist. But what is this leap? It is no longer a move toward a specific object of desire; rather, it has become a perhaps objectless breaking away from what the clown has been until now. He is motivated by nothing more definite than 'ma simple ivresse de renaître/Autre.' *Re*, the reiterative prefix, occurs three times in these two words. In the final version of 'Le Pitre châtié,' Mallarmé also increases both the structural visibility and the frequency of *re* as a terminal rhyme: the first and last verses of both quatrains end in *re* ('pénètre/fenêtre' had ended the second and third verses of the first quatrain in the earlier version, while 'traître' and 'hêtre' rhymed the first and fourth verses of the second quatrain), and a new rhyme in *re* is added in the tercets ('nacre' and 'sacre'). Reiterative and yet displaceable: except for 'renaître,' Mallarmé uses *re* not as a prefix but as an ending, thus modifying the sign of repetition with the suggestion (provided by the feminine ending) of indefinite extension. In *re*, we have, as it were, a floating reiterative: capable of being attached to almost any word, and of occupying different positions in different words. This lexical availability is analogous to what the clown seeks: an indeterminate repetition of his birth. Finally, such a rebirth is equivalent to death: to leap into a perpetually virginal being is to disappear into the thousand watery sepulchers which the clown 'innovates.' His incessant dying is his constant moving away from himself, his 'simple ivresse de renaître autre.'

This movement also describes the relation of the later version of 'Le Pitre châtié' to the earlier version. The latter is the poetic sepulcher in which the former's thematic contrasts disappear. It is our first example of what I will presently describe as Mallarmé's burial of poetry. The originality of 'Le Pitre châtié' is not that it replicates an already written poem, but it is nonetheless *by thinking the earlier version* that the poet produces a new version. The process of revising does not oppose a new work to the old work; so as long as the former does not exist, the latter will be abolished *as* it is being read – that is, as it is received into, in a sense replicated by, a receptive consciousness.

Revision could be taken as a model of criticism: in both cases, the work of art is annihilated by being embraced. Intimacy abolishes its object. It is perhaps this violent passivity which Henry James has in mind when, referring in his preface to *The Golden Bowl* to his revisions for the New York edition of his novels, he claims that the later versions are merely the 'only possible' vision he has of the earlier versions, and that revision is nothing more than 're-perusal, registered.'[23] The later text is the recording of an experience of the earlier text. The later version of 'Le Pitre châtié' could be read as a statement about what it was like to read the earlier version. It is as if Mallarmé's recording of his 're-perusal' of the latter resulted in a record of the poet-reader's 'simple ivresse' to have his poem be born again, no longer the same, as another. The later version would therefore be a self-reflexive movement which has as its object of reflection the exhilarating violation of the first poem. To 're-peruse' the clown's jump from love to art is to leap away from that jump; and, rather than merely substitute another thematic contrast for the one between the Muse and the woman, Mallarmé, in his new poem, 'replicates' the thematic leap with a poem about a leap from any definable being into mere, and radical otherness.

However, it is as if Mallarmé also repudiated his poetic leap in the

very act of accomplishing it. Both versions of 'Le Pitre châtié' end
on the sombre assertion that the clown's genius has been washed
away with his make-up. He has fled from 'la suie ignoble des
quinquets' (or, in the first version, 'notre baraque où fument [les]
quinquets [de la Muse]'); he has lost 'le suif de mes cheveux et le fard
de ma peau' in the lake; and his clown's costume has been left by
the trunk of the beech tree. The exhilarating nudity evoked in the
first tercet of both versions of the poem is bitterly equated with
sterility in the two conclusions of 'Le Pitre châtié.' The argument
made in the poem seems to be that artistic genius depends on certain
conventional accessories or accompaniments to artistic performance.
Outside the circus tent, without his costume and his make-up, the
clown in the first version is deprived of his genius; in the final version,
a sun-drenched rebirth becomes a 'rance nuit de la peau' when the
clown's make-up – which he equates with his artistic consecration – is
drowned in the glacier's treacherous waters. The disgust with
performance (with 'le mauvais Hamlet,' 'l'histrion qui du geste
évoquais/Comme plume la suie ignoble des quinquets') is accompanied by an apparent inability to formulate the performative innovations realized in the final version. The peculiarity of this position
is that it persists into Mallarmé's demonstration that art can be
created without a good deal of the 'make-up' of the first version. The
poet has not, it is true, leapt into a pure availability to language; but
in dropping the principal narrative ornamentation of the early
version – the reference to the woman, the address to the Muse – he
has effectively put into question the clown's simple equation of his
genius with the given conditions of his art.

The fable about art in 'Le Pitre châtié' is inadequate to the
innovative performance given in the later version of the poem.
To put this in another way, we might say that Mallarmé's betrayal
of the earlier version is itself betrayed by an anecdotal fidelity
of the revised poem to its model. The abolishing movement away
from the first 'Pitre châtié' is compensated for by a specular
movement at the end of the second version, a movement in which
revision is conservatively mythologized as replicative reflection.
Dislocation is qualified by relocation, and the latter bizarrely implies
a nostalgia for the conventional procedures of the first version.
Mallarmé sentimentally implies that the alternative to the esthetic
choices of his earlier poem is silence, whereas he has in fact begun
to show that he can leap through the 'canvas wall' of narrative,
thematic and psychological props, and continue to perform poetic-
ally. The disruptive play of such lines as 'Hilare or de cymbale à des

poings irrité' is not simply a disguise of the explicit statements of the first 'Pitre châtié.' That play *is* the meaning of the later version; far from giving greater dramatic immediacy to the clown's story, it makes the story itself an obsolete reminder of a dead person and a dead art.

2

POETRY IS BURIED

Appropriately enough, Mallarmé produces no poems at all for about six years following the announcement of his death in his letters of 1866 and 1867. So many unproductive years suggest a grave dilemma for Mallarmé's career as a writer: what kind of poetry can a dead poet produce? The *Correspondance* addresses this question rather optimistically, although it also records the devastating effect which Mallarmé's crisis has had on his capacity for writing anything at all. As late as 1869, Mallarmé's palpitations return even when he watches someone else write what he dictates, and he has only to take up his pen himself to fall prey to an attack of hysteria. And yet, with his personality gone, and with his resurrection as a 'sacred spider' ready to weave 'marvelous lacework' from the heart of a pre-existent Beauty, Mallarmé seems on the threshold of producing a work for which he might claim an extraordinary authority. If what is left of Stéphane Mallarmé continues to be shattered, rendered hysterical, by the very movements of his pen, such personal suffering is perhaps amply compensated for by Mallarmé's knowledge that the universe needs him as the site of its spiritual development. While he will no longer be the author of his work, he will, as it were, emit a Work of unparalleled significance.

Mallarmé even confides to his correspondents the number of volumes which will be produced, and the subject of each volume. To the brief descriptions of his projected work already quoted early in Chapter One, we might add the promise, in a letter to Catulle Mendès, of 'three or four volumes, unbending and miserly [opiniâtres et avares], which will be my life,' as well as the projected division of the work, in a letter sent about a year later to Cazalis, into one volume of Tales, one of Poetry, and another of Criticism (*C.*, pp. 324 and 342). What is the relation between a book conceived as the 'image' of the poet's development, and a work which documents 'the intimate correlations of Poetry with the Universe' (*C.*, pp. 242 and 259)? And how are we to reconcile the various structures which

25

Mallarmé proposes for his master-work? Does the later plan of three volumes (of Tales, Poetry, and Criticism) supersede an earlier plan according to which a volume on the discovery of the Beautiful would follow a volume on the discovery of Nothingness? But to point out such apparent inconsistencies is beside the point; unable, in any case, to guess what the unproduced Work might have been, we can stop at the fact – of no small significance in itself – that Mallarmé considers the death he speaks of in his letters not as the end of his literary career, but as the condition of literary productivity. Mallarmé's arrival in Paris in 1871, where, on the basis of a few poems seen by a few other writers, he is already welcomed as an authoritative voice in the world of letters, would seem to herald the start – after a long crisis of threatened sterility – of an exceptionally productive poetic career.

The protracted poetic silences in this career should not in themselves make us doubt the importance of the Work in Mallarmé's life. During the 1860s he was, after all, warning his friends that they would have to wait a long time before seeing the promised volumes. 'I need ten years,' Mallarmé writes to Cazalis in May 1867 (*C.*, p. 243). Four years later, in another letter to Cazalis, the time needed has doubled: 'In short, the mornings of twenty years' to finish the volumes of Tales, Poetry and Criticism (*C.*, p. 342). Furthermore, the end of the nineteenth century is, as Mallarmé notifies Verlaine in an autobiographical letter of 1885, an 'interregnum,' a time 'trop en désuétude et en effervescence préparatoire pour que [le poète] ait autre chose à faire qu'à travailler avec mystère en vue de plus tard ou de jamais.' The sign of the poet's understanding of his time is his detachment from it. He will occasionally send his contemporaries 'sa carte de visite, stances au sonnet, pour n'être point lapidé d'eux, s'ils le soupçonnaient de savoir qu'ils n'ont pas lieu.' Mallarmé's published poems would therefore be nothing more than strategic utterances, sounds made in order to gain time for a more authentic time. The calling card deceptively announces the passing presence of an absent poet to a public unwilling to see its own (apparent) existence as both outdated and unrealized. The poet's 'travail personnel,' as Mallarmé somewhat bizarrely calls it, 'sera anonyme, le Texte y parlant de lui-même et sans voix d'auteur.'[1] The authority of Mallarmé rests on the invisibility of a Work being prepared 'en vue de plus tard ou de jamais,' as well as on an inauthentic signature left with a nonexistent audience. There is only one Book, Mallarmé tells Verlaine: 'the orphic explanation of the Earth,' which everyone who has ever written has tried to produce, and which is 'the poet's only

26

duty' (*O.C.*, p. 663). Only the Text could claim to be *present*, but Presence, infinitely precious, has always been, perhaps always will be, indefinitely postponed.

Mallarmé could be treated as a primary example of literary imperialism in modern writing, of an effort – traceable, roughly, from Mallarmé to Jacques Lacan – to colonize an audience's interpretive ingenuities. The special, perhaps unbeatable twist which Mallarmé gives to this enterprise is to refer those ingenuities to an unwritten text. As Mallarmé criticism has shown, the hermeticism of the published work is not impenetrable; disagreements exist about the meanings of specific poems, but more or less plausible meanings have been proposed for every poem. The absent Presence of the Work, however, means that the critic's work can never be done. The notes *for* the Work assembled and published by Jacques Scherer[2] merely exacerbate this situation: they testify to the seriousness of Mallarmé's preparation for the Work (which he apparently intended to be read in front of an audience) without offering a single passage which can be said, with any certainty, to be part of the definitive Text. Thus speculative interpretation has nothing against which it may at least intermittently have the illusion of measuring itself. Certain interpretive limits are imposed merely by the given, final choice of words and verbal sequence in, say, the Baudelaire 'Tombeau' poem and the sonnet *A la nue accablante tu*. In the case of the Work, on the other hand, the objects which invite interpretation are not the objects *of* interpretation; in his letters and in his notes for the Book, Mallarmé directs the most strenuous exegetical efforts to an unfulfilled promise.

It would be difficult to imagine a more uncompromising exercise of literary authority. At the close of an exegetical lifetime, one may actually come to the end of *Finnegans Wake*. Mallarmé's verse and prose can certainly keep us occupied, but if we should happen to finish with them, there will always be the Work as the continuously receding, infinitely hypnotic horizon of further interpretation – or, more accurately, as the horizon of an interpretation which can never stop because *it has never been authorized to begin*. That withholding of authorization is perhaps Mallarmé's most astonishing gesture of control. But Mallarmé also derealizes the unrealized Text in a manner which deprives it of all authority. In his most imperialistic stance, Mallarmé implicitly defines the interpretation of his (written and unwritten) work as impossible and imperative; in another mood, he suggests that the insatiable interpretive activity which he unleashed is simply unnecessary. The discredited 'interregnum' gives Mallarmé the time to try out various modes of writing. Measured by the Work, all this activity is fundamentally dismissable. But perhaps *because of* its willed insignificance, it also allows Mallarmé to subvert his own narrative ordering of literary time and the consequent measuring of literary value in terms of an anticipatory (empty) designation of the climactic Masterwork.

Long after his own resurrection as a repository of universal Texts, Mallarmé remains fascinated by the deaths of other poets. The ambiguous nature of his fascination is disguised by the official form which it takes: Mallarmé's *Tombeaux* poems are memorializing tributes to the poets whose works they appear to honor. The first of these celebrations (and Mallarmé's first published poem since his arrival in Paris) is 'Toast funèbre,' Mallarmé's contribution to the *Tombeau de Théophile Gautier* (1873), a collection of pieces by eighty-three poets in honor of Gautier, who had died in October 1872. 'Toast funèbre' is perhaps most interesting as an extremely oblique dismissal of the poet to whom it pays tribute. Speaking of the piece in a letter to François Coppée, Mallarmé wrote: 'Je veux chanter, en rimes plates, une des qualités glorieuses de Gautier: le don mystérieux de voir avec les yeux (ôtez mystérieux). Je chanterai le voyant, qui, placé dans ce monde, l'a regardé, ce que l'on ne fait pas.'[3] What does it mean to know the world visually (a gift which may, or may not, be 'mysterious'...)? And how does poetic language express this ability to look?

The next-to-last stanza of 'Toast funèbre' problematizes the very gift which Mallarmé praises in his letter to Coppée. Using floral imagery which will be taken up again in the ironically doctrinal 'Prose pour des Esseintes' (written in 1884), Mallarmé distinguishes between the flowers of nature and the flowers of art. Only the latter guarantee the poet's immortality:

> Le Maître, par un œil profond, a, sur ses pas,
> Apaisé de l'éden l'inquiète merveille
> Dont le frisson final, dans sa voix seule, éveille
> Pour la Rose et le Lys le mystère d'un nom.
> Est-il de ce destin rien qui demeure, non?
> O vous tous, oubliez une croyance sombre.
> Le splendide génie éternel n'a pas d'ombre.
> Moi, de votre désir soucieux, je veux voir,
> A qui s'évanouit, hier, dans le devoir
> Idéal que nous font les jardins de cet astre,
> Survivre pour l'honneur du tranquille désastre

28

Poetry is buried

Une agitation solennelle par l'air
De paroles, pourpre ivre et grand calice clair,
Que, pluie et diamant, le regard diaphane
Resté là sur ces fleurs dont nulle ne se fane,
Isole parmi l'heure et le rayon du jour![4]

Two versions of naming are proposed in this stanza. The first is provided by the capitalization of Rose and Lys, and it suggests that poetic language is a form of idealization. This notion, by no means unimportant in Mallarmé, is treated more fully in the 'Prose pour des Esseintes,' where the poet boasts of establishing 'par la science/ L'hymne des cœurs spirituels [through knowledge/The hymn of spiritual hearts].' The Platonic Ideas mentioned in the exultant eighth stanza of that poem are visualized as a kind of magnification of natural forms.[5] The Idea of the gladiolus may be an 'immense' gladiolus, or, as the last line of 'Prose' perhaps wryly suggests, a 'too-big gladiolus.' In 'Toast funèbre,' the second version of naming is an exercise not in the transcendental doubling of nature in language (rose-as-object 'lifted up' into Rose), but an ingenious *mis*-naming. We may assume that 'pourpre ivre' alludes to a rose, and that 'grand calice clair' refers to a lily; continuing this translation, we could say that the poet's 'diaphanous look' is to his verbal flowers the equivalent of water and light ('pluie et diamant') for natural flowers. But what, exactly, do 'allude' and 'refer' mean here?

One is immediately tempted to call this type of allusiveness *précieux*; indeed, the word has frequently been applied to Mallarmé. *Précieux* misnaming is a coquettish linguistic puzzle. The speaker shies away from direct naming, and in earlier versions of *préciosité* in Europe, the verbal retreat does indeed seem to be motivated in part by a *pudeur* – a blend of shyness and repugnance – in front of 'natural' (especially material and sexual) realities. It is, however, also obvious that the *précieux* writer moves away from such realities in order to return to them – more exactly, in order to linger over them, to savor a somewhat aberrant way of designating them. There is a slightly wicked intellectual sensuality in *préciosité*: images of parts of the body, for example, are constantly *about to* enter the mind. Indeed, for the *précieux* audience, they are the reward for solving a verbal puzzle. In refusing to point directly at the physical, the *précieux* writer can detain it indefinitely on the threshold of our attention. It is not so much nature that he scorns as the vulgarity of immediate or climactic satisfactions. We should perhaps reverse the formulation that the *précieux* verbal puzzle is motivated by *pudeur* and say that *pudeur* is the psychological and moral alibi for the pleasure of transforming physical experience into sensually gratifying intellectual puzzles or play. If this is the case, the (anti-)interpretive rule (which is not to say the rule empirically obeyed) for the audience of a *précieux* performance would be to avoid figuring out the puzzle. The more adept one is at solving the *précieux* enigma, the more likely one is to destroy the dilatory *jouissance* peculiar to *préciosité*.

Epistemologically, this *jouissance* could be defined as the pleasure of not knowing. It is as if the *précieux* writer, in his misnomers, had literally missed the names of things. But his 'ignorance' is of course feigned: he could, after all, have directly named the parts of the body to which he alludes in more or less ingenious circumlocutions. Mallarmé's use of circumlocutions – an important source of his work's obscurity – is, on the contrary, related to a profound epistemological skepticism. If, on the one hand, he dreamt of a Book which would be so adequate to its subject that its language would be transparent to the phenomena which it describes, he also argued that language can produce only fictions. Deliberate misnaming is a strategic reminder of the intrinsic human inability to name or describe the world 'correctly.' For this strategy to be effective, it is not even necessary for periphrastic language to be untranslatable into a direct statement. 'Toast funèbre,' for example, ranges from the fairly clear substitution of 'pourpre ivre' and 'grand calice clair' for Rose and Lily, to the more obscure but still interpretable circumlocutions 'magique espoir du corridor' (for the hope for an afterlife) and 'Souvenirs d'horizons' (for Man). But even in proposing tentative translations designed to straighten out Mallarmé's oblique speech, we violate the spirit of his obliquity. For 'Toast funèbre' suggests that the value of poetry lies precisely in its exploiting the verbal productivity inherent in the act of misnaming.

The poet's 'diaphanous look' remains on his verbal flowers and not on the flowers of nature; furthermore, the former are isolated from the time and the light of the real day. If we take the 'hyperbolic' island evoked in 'Prose pour des Esseintes' as an image of nature transposed to art, Mallarmé's description of that island appears to suggest even more explicitly that poetic language is a kind of nonreferential naming.

> Oui, dans une île que l'air charge
> De vue et non de visions
> Toute fleur s'étalait plus large
> Sans que nous en devisions.

Telles, immenses, que chacune
Ordinairement se para
D'un lucide contour, lacune,
Qui des jardins la sépara.[6]

'Lacune' is in apposition to 'contour': the shapes of poetic language are also the gaps, the spaces, which separate poetry from material reality. In 'Prose,' Mallarmé gives us another version of an idea which we found, at the very beginning of this study, in one of his letters: poetry is a multiplication of distances. Poetic contours *are* sheer distance; 'the mystery of a name' is that it creates an interval between itself and the object (or thought) to which it presumably adheres in the act of naming.

Finally, the consciousness of these intervals produces not epistemological despair, but rather a joyous abstract sensuality. Just as the *précieux* enjoys the body in all the verbal strategies which he uses to approach, avoid, and surround it, so Mallarmé discovers the *jouissance* of real flowers in his linguistic misappropriations of them. 'Gloire du long désir, Idées': the ideas of poetry are the verbal fantasies of desire. The sign of desire is the energy of our fantasmatic movements away from the objects of desire. The intensely appetitive consciousness of the world oddly exceeds the things we might wish to name, as well, perhaps, as the ordering power of consciousness itself. As the adversary, skeptical 'Esprit de litige' is admonished in 'Prose pour des Esseintes,' the poet's silence should not be read as proof that the country of his mind didn't exist, but rather as the price of the dazzled disarray into which the ample luxuriance of imaginary contours has plunged him:

Oh! sache l'Esprit de litige,
A cette heure où nous nous taisons,
Que de lis multiples la tige
Grandissait trop pour nos raisons

Et non comme pleure la rive,
Quand son jeu monotone ment
A vouloir que l'ampleur arrive
Parmi mon jeune étonnement

D'ouïr tout le ciel et la carte
Sans fin attestés sur mes pas,
Par le flot même qui s'écarte,
Que ce pays n'exista pas.[7]

In 'Toast funèbre,' Gautier's apparent gift for seeing the world is implicitly treated as an anti-poetic illusion. And the stanza to which

I have been referring could be considered as part of a more general (yet always prudent) dismissal of Gautier. The poem begins, for example, with a firm rejection of any hope for an after-life:

> Salut de la démence et libation blême,
> Ne crois pas qu'au magique espoir du corridor
> J'offre ma coupe vide où souffre un monstre d'or![8]

Gautier the man is consigned to oblivion; more surprisingly, the poet does not even appear to survive in his own work. Gautier lives on in the homages of other poets: in the indirect homage of his disciples' works, and perhaps above all in the volume just published in his honor, in the poetic tribute of eighty-three writers which make up the *Tombeau de Théophile Gautier*:

> Et l'on ignore mal, élu pour notre fête
> Très simple de chanter l'absence du poëte,
> Que ce beau monument l'enferme tout entier.[9]

Displaced and dispersed, Gautier is, then, curiously removed from his own work. But not only is he placed 'tout entier' within a volume of other poets' tributes *to* him; Mallarmé also problematizes Gautier's presence in 'Toast funèbre' itself. In the stanza beginning 'Magnifique, total et solitaire,' the theme of Gautier's death is generalized into a reflection on men's 'false pride.' Gautier disappears into the 'haggard crowd' of mortal humanity, and the individual who answers the question asked by 'nothingness' at the end of the stanza is not a poet, but an anonymous dead man from another time (the 'Homme aboli de jadis'), merely one of the passers-by or one of those who have passed on into death ('Quelqu'un de ces passants').

'Toast funèbre' can, however, also be fairly unambiguous in its tribute to Gautier. The last stanza, for example, contrasts 'Le sépulcre solide où gît tout ce qui nuit,/Et l'avare silence et la massive nuit,'[10] with Gautier the 'pure poet' who defends his verse from the double threat of silence and blindness posed by death. Suggestions of a more complicated attitude toward the relation between seeing and writing poetry are dropped, and Gautier's vision is opposed to a massive nocturnal blindness – the harmful, anti-poetical night ('la nuit qui nuit') of biological death. The obscurity of 'Toast funèbre' may have less to do with the difficulty of specific verses than with the ultimately undecidable nature of Mallarmé's tribute to Gautier. And while Mallarmé can perhaps not help but be ironic about Gautier's presumed capacity to see the world objectively, the undecidability of 'Toast funèbre' does not derive essentially from the ambivalent feelings of one poet toward another. Mallarmé's relation to other poets would be inadequately described by Harold Bloom's analysis of the Oedipal ambivalences in writers' relations to the literary past. Mallarmé's relation to other poets is more abstract than anything this familial model allows for; it is an affectively impoverished relation, and perhaps because of that more fundamental than the Oedipal configurations.

Neither hostility nor attachment is especially evident in Mallarmé's tributes to Gautier, Baudelaire and Verlaine; rather, the poetic *hommage* provides the occasion for an emotionally and intellectually neutral moving away from the poets being honored, a movement which is the consequence of nothing more than the decision to make of them the object of a poem. Just as the project of naming the world results in the activity of *mis*naming, so the tributes to other poets inevitably become missed tributes. The *Tombeaux* poems are, by virtue of the very project which inspires them, *hommages manqués*. For Mallarmé, poetry is the dispersal of subjects; and it is as if its practice were therefore incompatible with the explicit monumentalizing intention of the *Tombeaux* poems, and perhaps even with any serious claim to the authority of a personal signature. Mallarmé's own initiation into writing, as we have seen, moves him away from himself, even leads him to announce his own death. The posthumous tribute is, for this always respectable man of letters, a satisfyingly oblique way of generalizing his experience of writing as the loss of authorship.

It would be possible to consider Mallarmé's other *Tombeaux* poems from a perspective similar to the one adopted here for 'Toast funèbre.' I am thinking, for example, of the importance of the tombstone itself in the poems honoring Poe and Verlaine. Poe's escape from the blasphemous hostilities of his contemporaries is a kind of posthumous petrification; he is generalized and capitalized by eternity into 'le Poëte' and 'Lui-même.' And the tercets, as Charles Mauron has noted, make Poe 'even more granite-like if that is possible.' The quatrains refer to a historically recognizable poet, but in the tercets neither Poe nor Mallarmé himself is present except in the stones which contain or express them. Mallarmé will 'sculpt' a 'bas-relief' depicting the hostility of earth and heaven, and Poe's tomb suddenly becomes a mysterious extra-terrestrial presence. The astonishing suggestion that his tombstone has fallen to earth as a result of some obscure cosmic disaster – 'Calme bloc ici-bas chu d'un désastre obscur' – evokes, as Mauron writes, an immense and empty plain, a wholly non-human landscape.[11] The disaster of Poe's life is curiously transmuted into a barely guessed-at catastrophe in outer space, one that has the effect, in the poem, of wiping the slate clean of human presences. In 'Toast funèbre,' the poet was dispersed both in the works of dozens of other poets (including the dispersing 'Toast funèbre' itself), and in the anonymous crowd of the dead. In 'Le Tombeau d'Edgar Poe,' the very tombstone – 'tombe,' 'bloc,' 'granit' – meant to commemorate Poe's life (or Mallarmé's commemorative relief *on* that tombstone) is a cosmic rock which both protects the poet from the 'black flights' of future Blasphemy and effectively trivializes *all* human references.

Finally, the 1897 'Tombeau' poem for the first anniversary of Verlaine's death subtly suggests Verlaine's complicity in his own invisibility. Once again, death becomes the occasion for evoking non-human landscapes: the quatrains rather obscurely refer to the tombstones in the Batignolles cemetery where Verlaine is buried, as well perhaps as to the 'immaterial mourning' of a ringdove's warbling and the passing of a cloud in front of a star. The first tercet – interestingly enough for our purposes – asks, not even: where is Verlaine? but rather: who is looking for Verlaine? 'He is hidden in the grass, Verlaine' – as if the poet were shying away from his own tombstone, were trying to get out of the way of the 'angered black rock' of the first verse. Verlaine, alone among the poets honored in the *Tombeaux* series, *removes himself* from the principal scene of Mallarmé's homage. In the final tercets, Mallarmé uses the word perhaps most frequently associated with Verlaine's sensibility – 'naïvement' – and yet he perhaps also recognized that Verlainean naïveté is the poet's most sophisticated strategy for hiding himself. Eléonore Zimmermann has shown that the simple, direct, unproblematically confessional Verlaine is only one aspect of an impressive virtuosity of poetic voice; Verlaine is no more 'in' 'Chanson d'automne' than in such psychologically and erotically sophisticated poems as 'Crimen amoris' or 'Vendange.'[12]

Mallarmé's affection for Verlaine – discreetly transparent in 'notre vagabond,' in the gentle 'Verlainean' repetition of the poet's name in verse 11, and in the generous 'saving' of Verlaine, in the second tercet, from his own somber, Catholic view of death – may have included the recognition that, for all the obvious differences between Verlaine's work and his own, the former was himself a model of the psychological subject's dispersal, or even death, in his writing. The moments of sentimental self-effacement in Verlaine's verse derive from a self-effacement inherent in the act of writing itself. Verlaine's slightly funny hiding in the Mallarmé poem honoring him (a hiding which might be contrasted with Poe's monumental visibility in the first stanza of the better known 'Tombeau d'Edgar Poe') anecdotally refers us to the timid persona in Verlaine's verse; more radically, it assimilates Verlaine himself to the Mallarméan project of using poetic celebration as a means of burying the poet, of helping him to disappear from the field of writing.

But the consequences of Mallarmé's death are by no means limited to the burial of other poets. Even more astonishingly, alongside this depersonalizing intention we may detect strategies and arguments designed to bury poetry itself as a prelude to the play of fictions. In the lecture which he gave at Oxford and Cambridge in 1894, and which was published the following year under the title 'La Musique et les lettres,' Mallarmé begins by announcing the 'most surprising' news, news of an unprecedented phenomenon: 'On a touché au vers.' But his remarks on the debate in France over the *vers libre* – which is the evidence given for this meddling with verse – quickly lead to more fundamental considerations. For in the quarrels over prosody, 'l'acte d'écrire se scruta jusqu'en l'origine,' and the subject of Mallarmé's lecture has become 'plus vaste...que telle rénovation de rites et de rimes.'[13] Somehow implicit in a debate about versification is a doubt about the very possibility of writing: 'A savoir s'il y a lieu d'écrire.' Is there any reason to write, is there any place for writing? Or, to approach the subject from the perspective of an even more radical doubt: 'Quelque chose comme les Lettres existe-t-il?' (*O.C.*, pp. 643–5). Beyond or before questions about the nature and value of literature is an uncertainty about whether it *can* exist.

We may consider this question by asking, first of all, why Mallarmé asks it. To wonder if literature exists, and where and to what purpose the act of writing can take place, would seem to be a strategic prelude to a definition of literature's specificity. Indeed, Mallarmé appears to be moving in this direction when he suggests that he is referring to something different from 'l'affinement, vers leur expression burinée, des notions, en tout domaine.' An architect, for example, might be said to produce literature when he 'completes' his buildings by re-presenting them as discourse. They had begun as an idea, and they are perfected as an idea: '...tout ce qui émane de l'esprit, se réintègre.' But this, apparently, is not the type of specificity which Mallarmé has in mind. And yet literature, like the architect's discourse, is a turning back of the mind upon itself. It is not, however, the 'engraving' of notions which can affect the external world. Mallarmé is very clear about this: 'La nature a lieu, on n'y ajoutera pas....' The architect and the doctor, on the contrary, do add to nature. It is as if, in asserting the impossibility of any such additions, Mallarmé were attempting to link the specificity of literature to a special and extreme type of impotence. The architect's discourse is disqualified as literature by virtue of its capacity to affect material reality. Even more: Mallarmé implicitly denies the statue of any reality at all to literature. 'Nous savons, captifs d'une formule absolue que, certes, n'est que ce qui est.' Literature is a 'fiction' and the principal part of the literary mechanism is 'nothing.' Nonetheless, Mallarmé astonishingly maintains (while warning his audience that this is an 'exaggeration') that literature does exist 'et si l'on veut, seule, à l'exception de tout' (*O.C.*, pp. 645–7).[14] On the one hand, nothing exists *but* literature. On the other hand, not only does writing take place without, somehow, having a place; more radically, writing *is not*.

I wish to stress the extreme nature of this position before considering Mallarmé's attempt to define the unlocatable, inexistent yet omnipresent place of literature. Just how far Mallarmé is willing to go in his repudiation of literature's function and existence is even clearer in 'Crise de vers,' a piece which has a thrillingly frivolous speculative mobility in its disparate messages about its own subject. The essay, published in *Divagations* (an 1897 collection of Mallarmé's work in prose), combines passages from several prose pieces: a few revised pages from an article published as 'Averses ou critique' in the series of monthly articles entitled *Variations sur un sujet*, articles which appeared in *La Revue Blanche* in 1895; several paragraphs from 'Vers et musique en France,' which appeared in March 1892 in *The National Observer*; a few passages from the collection *Vers et prose* (1893); a paragraph originally in 'La Musique et les lettres'; and the main section of Mallarmé's 1886 foreword to René Ghil's *Traité du verbe*. Certain discontinuities in 'Crise de vers' are a function of the essay's patchwork quality. (Even the pages from *Variations sur un sujet* are not given continuously; they form three separate blocks in 'Crise de vers.') However, the result, far from being something exceptional in Mallarmé, exemplifies Mallarmé's most characteristic procedures. 'Crise de vers' is a piece of poetic theory, but its own organization tells us more about the Mallarméan esthetic than any of its specific statements. Indeed, 'Crise de vers' is a crucial document for the study of Mallarmé's disappearance as a thinker interested in, or perhaps even capable of, the very activity of making statements.

What is the crisis referred to by Mallarmé's title? Is it that 'breaking' of French verse which Mallarmé dates from Hugo's death, the substitution of a 'polymorphous' meter for both the classical and the romantic alexandrines? Or is it a question of a more fundamental and permanent epistemological crisis, the absence of a 'supreme' language which would 'materially' express 'truth'? Mallarmé connects the prosodic innovations of his time to a crisis 'dans nos circonstances mentales vierges' (*O.C.*, p. 365). But the exact nature of these 'virgin' circumstances remains problematic in the essay. One possibility would be to consider the crisis of the alexandrine as allowing for an unprecedented universalizing of poetry. The *vers libre* would be nothing less than the rhythmic modulations imposed on language by individual souls. '...Toute âme,' as Mallarmé had written in 'La Musique et les lettres,' 'est un noeud rythmique' (*O.C.*, p. 644). Verse *is* literature, and we have verse as soon as diction is accentuated, or as soon as language is cadenced.[15] A noteworthy and logical consequence of 'polymorphous' rhythm is that, for the first time, 'au cours de l'histoire littéraire d'aucun peuple, concurremment aux grandes orgues générales et séculaires, où s'exalte, d'après un latent clavier, l'orthodoxie, quiconque avec son jeu et son ouïe individuels se peut composer un instrument, dès qu'il souffle, le frôle ou frappe avec science; en user à part et le dédier aussi à la Langue' (*O.C.*, p. 363).[16]

From this perspective, the crisis of 'Crise de vers' would be the democratization of poetry. Literature exists 'alone, to the exclusion of everything else,' because it is no longer a specialized activity; the 'science' of poetry is equivalent to a kind of self-possession through self-attunement. Furthermore, there are no longer interruptions or dead periods in the history of poetry. French poetry, Mallarmé writes, has been 'intermittent' until now. Periods of 'extinction, plutôt usure à montrer la trame, redites,' follow '[d'] orgiaques excès pérodiques.' But with the collapse of classical verse and the devaluation of rhyme as a primary source of poetic 'enchantment,' '...la retrempe, d'ordinaire cachée, s'exerce publiquement, par le recours à de délicieux à-peu-près' (*O.C.*, p. 361).[17] The possibility of an exhaustion of literary forms has become historically obsolete, since form itself has become the visible play, in language, of an individual's 'rhythmic knot.'

If, however, poetry can now be produced everywhere all the time, Mallarmé also qualifies this poetic explosion as 'jeux à côté' or marginal games, and, as we have just seen, delightful approximations. When someone plays an instrument 'built with his individual technique and ear,' his use of that instrument is 'à part.' That is, the universalizing of poetry is, curiously enough, always to the side of both Language and the 'orthodoxy' of the consecrated 'organ' of classical verse. The music of individual souls is not played on the major instruments. The suggestion that the modern period has discovered the essence of poetry by refusing to define rhythm except in terms of the modulations and pressures of individual sensibilities is countered by a hint that the games of modern verse may be simply the workshop in which some future use of the orthodox keyboard is being prepared. The laboratory in which French poetry is periodically refreshed and refurbished has become a visible scene of French poetry.

The crisis, we begin to suspect, may be descriptive as well as historical. Mallarmé asks us to imagine poetry as simultaneously universal, historically continuous, approximate, and marginal. The conceptual ferment at work here is intensified when, further on in 'Crise de vers,' Mallarmé speaks of an 'œuvre pure [qui] implique la disparition élocutoire du poète, qui cède l'initiative aux mots.' A certain universalizing of poetry is still seen as the work of the modern period, but it is no longer a question of everyone producing poetry from a unique 'rhythmic knot.' We can no longer be stirred by the democratizing prospect of multiple sensibilities translating themselves into multiple poetic rhythms; rather, the last quarter of a century, Mallarmé writes, has been visited by 'quelque éclair absolu [some absolute flash of lightning]' which has awakened the dream of a perfectly anonymous art. Contemporary youth 'bégaya le magique concept de l'Œuvre.' According to this concept, there would be only one book: 'au monde, sa loi... La différence, d'un ouvrage à l'autre, offrant autant de leçons proposées dans un immense concours pour le texte véridique, entre les âges dits civilisée ou – lettrés' (*O.C.*, pp. 366–7).[18]

Mallarmé speaks of a parallel between the symmetry of verses within a poem and the 'authentic' placing of that poem within a volume; but this symmetry also 'vole, outre le volume, à plusieurs inscrivant, eux, sur l'espace spirituel, le paraphe amplifié du génie, anonyme et parfait comme une existence d'art' (*O.C.*, p. 367).[19] The artistic existence is, then, the precise opposite of a state in which each individual plays out his own 'rhythmic knot.' Mallarmé calls this notion of an anonymous and perfect stamp of genius a 'chimera'; the idea is itself a sign of crisis, and it calls forth the energetic imagery of the modern period having been struck by 'quelque éclair absolu.' (Characteristically, however, this storm is immediately domesticated, transformed into the rain streaming down the window-panes of Mallarmé's library.) We have thus moved from a multiplication of poetry to the 'flight' of poetry outside all volumes of verse. Mallarmé's contemporaries have, from this perspective, initiated a sort of cataclysmic depersonalization of verse. According to 'the magic concept of the Work,' the works of individual poets will be points of intersection inscribed in a 'spiritual space.' Considered alone, a book is a waste-product of self-expression, a product of psychological and historical chance. But its 'ordering' or 'symmetry' transcends its existence. The relations among the most apparently self-expressive elements of a single work are determined by psychologically non-expressive affinities; *the author is omitted by his structure.*

But this position is by no means privileged in 'Crise de vers.' It is frictionally juxtaposed not only with a view of poetry as the music of individual souls, but also with other (non-structural *and* non-psychological) notions of art. For example, if the passage from which I have just been quoting (taken mainly from *Variations sur un sujet*) suggests that the modern period has taken a decisive step in the 'immense concours pour le texte véridique,' a text which would be the world's law, an even more famous paragraph in 'Crise de vers' (from the same piece in *Variations sur un sujet*) should undoubtedly be read as conveying the opposite message. I am thinking of the passage beginning 'Les langues imparfaites en cela que plusieurs, manque la suprême,' in which Mallarmé suggests that verse exists because language can never 'materially' be 'truth'. Verse is what Mallarmé calls a 'superior complement' which philosophically makes up for ('rémunère') the permanent, incurable defect of human languages. This, I believe, is not at all the same thing as saying that books have value only to the extent that they point, however falteringly, to the composition of the Work. On the one hand, the fact that words do not have thought's transparency to truth leads Mallarmé to devalue language. To think is 'écrire sans accessoires, ni chuchotement mais tacite encore l'immortelle parole.' But the verbal expression of thought renders thought opaque. In one sense Mallarmé views language as an epistemological disaster. His references to a poetry composed of silences, of the spaces between words, can in part be understood as a consequence of the secondary status given to words. Language is a fall from thought; a priority, at once ontological and epistemological, is accorded to a non-verbal thought capable, without mediation, of knowing the universe. Mallarmé nostalgically imagines an equation in which to think the universe (to receive and to emit it) would be to realize its structure. On the other hand – and this superficially more modest concept is, as we shall see, considerably more difficult to grasp – language has a superiority directly related to its epistemological incompetence. Poetic language does not make up for the deficiencies of ordinary language, and, in spite of a perhaps unfortunately celebrated passage in which Mallarmé 'regrette que le discours défaille à expliquer les objets par des touches y repondant en coloris ou en allure,' nothing suggests that he proceeded from this regret to an actual effort to correct the presumed linguistic defect which, to use his famous example, lends dark tones to the word referring to 'day' in French – 'jour' – and light tones to the word designating 'night' – 'nuit' (*O.C.*, pp. 363–4).[20]

Maurice Blanchot has pointed out the irrelevance of knowledge to the Mallarméan idea of literature. Mallarmé refers to his 'said flower' – 'Je dis: une fleur!' – as 'quelque chose d'autre que les calices sus.' His voice relegates the outlines of the real flower to oblivion, and in its place, 'musicalement se lève, idée même et suave, l'absente de tous bouquets.' One might of course interpret this 'absent' flower to be the idea of the flower found in nature. The act of speaking would thus remove us from visible outlines, would do away with what Mallarmé calls (in the paragraph just preceding the one beginning 'Je dis: une fleur!') 'la gêne d'un proche ou concret rappel,' in order to give us 'la notion pure' (*O.C.*, p. 368).[21] We might then have a perfect correspondence between the flower and an epistemologically accurate idea of it. Some of Mallarmé's statements appear to move in this direction, but we should remember that the spoken flower is something different not merely from real flowers but also from *known* flowers – that is, precisely from what we might have thought the verbal flower to be. Poetry gives us neither nature nor knowledge of nature.[22] In the same way that the poet's evoking 'the mystery of a name' turns out to be an activity of misnaming in 'Toast funèbre,' the musical idea which rises in the place vacated by real flowers in the passage from 'Crise de vers' appears immediately to separate itself from all bouquets. It realizes what Mallarmé calls in the last paragraph of 'Crise de vers' 'l'isolement de la parole,' a phrase which should remind us of the isolation from nature of the 'solemn agitation' of words in 'Toast funèbre,' as well as of the 'lucide contour, lacune' which, in 'Prose pour des Essientes,' separates the imaginary flowers from all real gardens.

We have not finished with the speculative wandering of 'Crise de vers.' More specifically, we have still to define what the ambiguous superiority of verse consists of. If Mallarmé denies epistemological value to poetry, he also has nothing but scorn for a defense of poetry as communication. As far as the exchange of human thoughts is concerned, it would probably suffice, Mallarmé writes, 'de prendre

ou de mettre dans la main d'autrui en silence une pièce de monnaie'
(*O.C.*, p. 368).[23] Thus, even when he appears to propose an esthetic
which would favor a view of art as communication, Mallarmé
dismisses communication. The democratization of poetry which I
referred to earlier in connection with the notion that 'every soul is
a melody,' that to make language respond to this individual music
is to produce poetry, could easily inspire a vision of a universal
human community through art. Proust, for example, is inspired by
just such a vision. Art gives us the 'real residue' of personality, the
particular essence of a self. Original composers, writes the narrator
of *A la Recherche du temps perdu*, keep returning to 'a unique
accent... which is a proof of the irreducibly individual existence of
the soul.' Art enables us 'to know that essential quality of another
person's sensations into which love for another person does not allow
us to penetrate.' The anguish of human isolation is surmounted only
by the transparency of the work of art, which makes visible 'that
intimate composition of those worlds which we call individual
persons and which, without the aid of art, we should never know.'[24]

In part, the Proustian esthetic is an esthetic of compensation, even
of consolation. Psychically fractured and tortured by the impenetra-
bility of others in life, the Proustian narrator finds both personal
unity and communion with others through art. The idea is sentimentally appealing, but it remains unexamined in Proust. Is there,
for example, nothing problematic about the notion of an esthetic
medium expressing 'individual persons'? What is the relation between a person and, say, a musical phrase or a painted seascape?
Would Marcel feel that he finally possesses Albertine if he were able
to hear that 'unique accent' which, in Vinteuil's music, gives him
access to the composer's irreducibly individual spiritual existence?
What is the relation between the hidden desires of others (desires
which torture Marcel in his fruitless efforts to appropriate others),
and the uniqueness of literary or musical accents?

Perhaps because the linear structure of *A la Recherche du temps
perdu* is that of an epistemological detective story, art is, in a sense,
condemned to solve problems which are irrelevant to it. We follow
the philosophical drama of Marcel's efforts to penetrate the external
world. From the *drame du coucher* to the young Marcel's frustrated
attempts to learn the secrets of nature, to the demonstrated impossibility of knowing others in friendship, in love, and in social life, we
move from defeat to defeat until, finally, the narrator realizes that
only art gives access to others. The narrative satisfaction which this
offers to both the reader and Marcel perhaps makes it easy to forget

that the mental events 'inscribed' in a sonata are incomparable to, say, the inferred movements of lesbian desire. There is no reason to believe that the part of another individual's experience with which we have contact in a work of art is the part hidden from us in love or social life. The universalizing of artistic creation 'solves' the problem of human communication only within the area *created by* the production of art.

Mallarmé, unconstrained in his poetic theory by the epistemological suspense which helps Proust to unify his massive, potentially disconnected novelistic enterprise, can equate poetic talent with a kind of self-concentration without concluding that poetry communicates a self. The instrument made from an individual's 'individual technique and ear' is 'dedicated' to Language. The individuality expressed in poetry is an event of linguistic inflection rather than of psychological depth. The communication of feelings or of sensibilities is reduced by Mallarmé to an elementary fiscal exchange, or to banal, unproblematic reporting. We might add that the very concept of such communication simplifies the exchange of human thought by its inherently vulgar version of mental movements. The 'rhythmic knot' in individuals is not a psychic enigma. Rather, psychic enigmas are, so to speak, the demusicalizing of that knot, its reduction to the status of reportable fact, or movable currency.

Thus, from a Mallarméan point of view, the universalizing of poetry, far from realizing a dream of human community, makes obsolete the very nostalgia for such a community by virtue of the depersonalizing medium in which it is realized. Depersonalizing and de-realizing: the self undergoes an ontological regression in poetry, it recedes into virtuality and becomes a play of fictions. Mallarmé uses these terms to describe the 'receding' of speech itself in poetry: 'Au contraire d'une fonction de numéraire facile et représentatif, comme le traite d'abord la foule, le dire, avant tout, rêve et chant, retrouve chez le Poëte, par nécessité constitutive d'un art consacré aux fictions, sa virtualité' (*O.C.*, p. 368).[25] In poetry, language reports on neither the world nor a self; it is removed, we might say, from both its epistemological function and its numismatic status. The individual 'melodies' communicated by a universalizing of poetic production, far from publicizing the 'essential quality of another person's sensations,' perhaps express nothing more 'essential' than a certain tempo of availability *to* sensation, the rhythm with which various modes of being are abandoned, moved away from, fictionalized.

'Crise de vers' illustrates this process through the speculative restlessness with which Mallarmé moves among different theoretical positions. I have not yet mentioned the ambiguity of the Mallarméan notion of poetry's allusiveness. The different contemporary schools of poetry, Mallarmé notes, all agree in refusing 'les matériaux naturels et, comme brutale, une pensée exacte les ordonnant; pour ne garder de rien que la suggestion.' This idea, which we have encountered in Mallarmé's correspondence, is also taken up in a paragraph from 'La Musique et les lettres' reproduced in 'Crise de vers.' Literary art deals in allusion and suggestion; its 'sortilège,' or magic charm, is to liberate, 'hors d'une poignée de poussière ou réalité sans l'enclore, au livre, même comme texte, la dispersion volatile soit l'esprit, qui n'a que faire de rien outre la musicalité de tout.' But in the same section of 'Crise de vers,' Mallarmé speaks of the esthetic error of claiming to include 'au papier subtil du volume autre chose que par exemple l'horreur de la forêt, ou le tonnerre muet épars au feuillage; non le bois intrinsèque et dense des arbres' (*O.C.*, pp. 365–6).[26] What is the relation between a rendering of 'the musicality of everything' and a rendering of the effects or the atmosphere of things? Is it the same thing to transcribe our impression of a forest and to describe the forest itself indirectly and allusively?

Most ambiguous of all is the notion of musicality. Which of the positions just outlined is most consistent with a rendering of 'the musicality of everything'? As Suzanne Bernard has pointed out, music for Mallarmé is at times primarily a matter of sounds in poetry (for example, the alliterations, assonances, and other patterns of sound repetitions in *Hérodiade*), and at other times it refers to the 'rhythm between relationships.'[27] In the last paragraph of 'Crise de vers,' the distinctive nature of poetry appears to be linked to its incantatory language. A verse creates a new 'total word' from its several individual words, a word 'étranger à la langue et comme incantatoire [foreign to language like an incantation].' The 'isolement de la parole' in poetry is not only, as I have said, an isolating of language from nature, but also a separation of language *from itself*, the creation of new linguistic units on the basis of sound. But, more often in 'Crise de vers,' we are dealing with the relational notion of music. Toward the end of the essay, for example, Mallarmé associates the breaking up of traditional literary rhythms which he had discussed earlier to 'un art d'achever la transposition, au Livre, de la symphonie ou uniment de reprendre notre bien: car, ce n'est pas de sonorités élémentaires par les cuivres, les cordes, les bois, indéniablement mais de l'intellectuelle parole à son apogée que doit avec plénitude et évidence, résulter, en tant que l'ensemble des rapports existant dans tout, la Musique' (*O.C.*, pp. 367–8).[28] This second version of poetic music is significantly different from the first. We have moved from an emphasis on the incantatory qualities of language to what might be called a strategic use of a musical metaphor in order to *abolish* sound from poetry. The 'exchange' between music and literature which Mallarmé announces in 'La Musique et les lettres' creates a music alien to the sound of music, one without 'le tumulte des sonorités' (*O.C.*, pp. 648–9). There are extremely elusive, undeveloped, and crucial connections between Mallarmé's appeal to music, his emphasis on silence, and the relational esthetic which comes to dominate, even to obsess his thought. The central element in this complex network is the claim that what matters in literature is not specific statements or images, but rather the structural constellation of a work. The logic behind this emphasis is most clearly formulated in 'La Musique et les lettres.' 'La Nature a lieu, on n'y ajoutera pas'; therefore, for the poet, 'tout l'acte disponible, à jamais et seulement, reste de saisir les rapports, entre temps, rares ou multipliés....'[29] At the 'intersections' of these relational systems, the poet will place, simply as a 'décor' or scenery, 'l'ambiguité de quelques figures belles [the ambiguity of a few beautiful figures]' (*O.C.*, 647–8). Poetic figures are thus reduced to an ornamental role, or, perhaps, at most, to the functional role of structural supports. If they are necessary to maintain the structure, the structural design takes place *between* them.

Finally, Mallarmé hesitates between thinking of this design as the world's law (or the universe's spiritual development), as an impersonal linguistic phenomenon (words take the initiative away from the poet), and, finally, as the spatialization of an individual's internal melody. The esthetics of 'Crise de vers' and of 'La Musique et les lettres' is itself a speculative design *between* these positions. 'Les rapports, entre temps, rares et multipliés' are, for example, grasped 'd'après quelque état intérieur et que l'on veuille à son gré étendre, simplifier le monde.' Relations perceived *in* the world are thus the structuralizing simplification of the world according to a subjective design. 'La totale arabesque' which establishes connections among all the 'figures belles' of a literary work is a 'chiffration mélodique tue, de ces motifs qui composent une logique, avec nos fibres' (*O.C.*, pp. 647–8).[30]

The speculative restlessness which I have been documenting is perhaps the major 'statement' of Mallarmé's theoretical writing. We might of course have strained toward proposing a conceptual unity for 'Crise de vers,' a unity to which Mallarmé himself, however, seems indifferent. Instead, by emphasizing the mobility of Mallarmé's conceptual performance, I have wanted to suggest that his essay never achieves the status of a secure and privileged statement *about* his work. It is an exemplification rather than a privileged summary of his esthetic, and it therefore must be treated *nonreductively* but as a *symptomatic* text. If we read it in this way, we will, I think, come to see that 'Crise de vers' is at odds with some of Mallarmé's most ambitious claims for literature. The frequently disorienting ease with which Mallarmé's thought *moves* in 'Crise de vers' suggests that literature's peculiar nature may have to do with a certain type of restlessness or moving away from its own statements. In spite of the theoretical tensions in both pieces, 'Crise de vers' and 'La Musique et les lettres,' as we have seen, do recurrently disparage literature's claiming to do or to be anything else. According to the strain of Mallarmé's thought most nearly adequate to his performances as a writer, literature would be an essentially wordless fiction incapable both of communicating the nature of reality and of producing knowledge of reality. For all the extraordinary claims which Mallarmé makes for literature, he also defines it as an unlocatable – perhaps even unheard and unseen – activity devoid of any semiotic or epistemological authority. We might even define Mallarmé's major enterprise – astonishing as this may seem – as an effort to do away with literature. He comes to be engaged, as I have wished to show in this chapter, in the somewhat eerie strategy of celebrating writers and literature as a way of burying them.

And yet Mallarmé does not give up writing. In fact, he begins what I take to be his subversion of literature at the very moment when he becomes a public man of letters. I would define his most original work from the early seventies on (after his move to Paris) as a continuously renewed effort to save writing from those very claims for literature, for the Work, which he himself frequently makes. An important implication of this enterprise is a certain equalization of different types of writing. In spite of Mallarmé's deprecation of his published work in the 1885 autobiographical letter to Verlaine, he also authorizes us to think of all his work (not only the poems and the consecrated prose pieces on artistic subjects, but also *La Dernière mode*, *Les Mots anglais* and even the *Contes indiens*) as a persistently ironic comment on the unrealized Book. That is, Mallarmé's published work should not be subordinated to a projected absolute Work; nor should it be thought of as a kind of desperate admission of the Work's impossibility. The Work may be no less peripheral in his career than his unquestionably peripheral works.... If we speak of Mallarmé's revolutionary position in the history of literature, it may be precisely those qualities which make his writing seem hopelessly remote from the Book as an 'orphic explanation of the Earth' which define his most revolutionary accomplishment.

Mallarmé's reputation has both profited and suffered from his being associated with a mystique of creative scarcity and even sterility. His silences are in fact highly ambiguous. While it is striking, for example, that he produced no new poem from 1866 to 1873, and while we may legitimately be astonished to learn that he seems to have written only two poems (the 'Tombeau d'Edgar Poe' and the sonnet beginning *Sur les bois oubliés*) between 'Toast funèbre' (1873) and 'Prose pour des Esseintes' (1884), Mallarmé, especially after settling in Paris, was engaged in an extraordinary diversity of literary projects. And while an occasional letter after 1871 continues to promote the notion of literary hierarchy by suggesting that only the unwritten Work counts, that the rest is only 'calling cards' or responses to material need, Mallarmé hardly seems to have distributed his energies in a way consistent with such a hierarchy of literary seriousness. In this respect, Mallarmé's career is very different from Joyce's and even from that of his disciple Valéry. No single compositional activity seems to have occupied or *held* Mallarmé as *Ulysses* and *Finnegans Wake* held and centered Joyce. We do not even have anything analogous to the volumes of Valéry's *Cahiers* – that is, to consistently pursued and transcribed reflections, over a period of years, on the nature of art and on the mechanism of thought. For the purposes of 'high culture,' Mallarmé promised much and produced little, and he could be, indeed has been criticized for the meager evidence he left of his concentration on a masterwork, and for the apparent ease with which he dropped his work on the Book and composed all the articles for eight issues of a women's fashion magazine or inscribed humorous quatrains on the eggs which he offered his friends at Easter.

But the very frivolousness detectable in Mallarmé's career as a man of letters can also be approached as the external professional sign of a radical reassessment of writing as a *value* of culture. To legislate the literary quality of *La Dernière mode* or to rehabilitate *Les Contes indiens* for 'serious' study would be to miss the spirit of that reassessment, and I will therefore not be submitting Mallarmé's 'minor' works to critical analysis. It will perhaps be more profitable merely to register our sense of Mallarmé's restless availability to various sorts of projects, of the ease with which he moved among diverse modes of writing. We should then be prepared to search not for clues to what the Book might have been, but rather for the critical terms in which to describe our own encounter with an intense, even voracious, and yet disarmingly light sociability.

3

IGITUR, THE POET
WRITES

Almost everything Mallarmé wrote during the last twenty-five years of his life was 'occasional,' in response to particular solicitations of all sorts. There were of course the financial pressures: 'J'ai dû faire,' Mallarmé wrote to Verlaine, 'dans des moments de gêne ou pour acheter de ruineux canots, des besognes propres, et voilà tout (Dieux Antiques, Mots Anglais) dont il sied de ne pas parler....' Although Mallarmé goes on to claim that '...à part cela les concessions aux nécessités comme aux plaisirs n'ont pas été fréquentes,' his work actually seems full of such 'concessions' (*O.C.*, p. 663).[1] I am thinking, for example, of the 100 pages in the Pléiade edition labelled *Vers de circonstance*: the ingeniously rhymed quatrains written on Easter eggs and fans or accompanying New Year's Day gifts of candied fruit, the versified addresses on the envelopes of notes sent to dozens of acquaintances, the short pieces composed for a baptism, for the inaugural evening of the *Revue indépendante*, for Mallarmé's barber, for the walls of an outdoor privy in the country....

Even much of the 'serious' poetry is circumstantial: not only the *Hommages et Tombeaux* series, but also the *Eventail* poems and the *Feuillets d'album* (which include sonnets and rondeaux addressed to Méry Laurent as well as the remarkable 'Remémoration d'amis belges,' Mallarmé's tribute to his hosts in Bruges during his 1890 visit to Belgium, where he lectured on Villiers de l'Isle-Adam). Finally, Mallarmé's prose writing, even more frequently than his verse, bears the mark of circumstantial performance. He composed prefaces to books by other writers, and we have several pages of toasts in honor of other poets. The important piece 'La Musique et les lettres' is essentially the lecture he gave at Oxford and Cambridge. In *Quelques médaillons et portraits en pied*, the 1896 essay on Verlaine is the speech Mallarmé gave at Verlaine's funeral; the Rimbaud piece of the same year was commissioned by the American magazine *The Chap Book*; and the short study of Théodore de Banville was written for the unveiling, in 1892, of the monument to Banville in the Luxembourg gardens. Finally, most of the essays on theater and ballet which Mallarmé grouped under the heading *Crayonné au théâtre* in the prose collection *Divagations* first appeared as articles in *La Revue indépendante*. Another journal, *La Revue blanche*, published ten essays in a series of monthly pieces entitled *Variations sur un sujet*. The circumstances just referred to vary considerably: from private messages to Méry Laurent to a book on the English language designed for use in schools and presumably undertaken for financial reasons, or to the contractual obligations of journalistic commissions. The contingency of Mallarmé's writing is none the less striking. How are we to think of this contingency? On the one hand, Mallarmé would probably want us to see it as a sign of the 'interregnum,' of a time when the serious writer invisibly prepares the Work and sends 'calling cards' (for example, circumstantial verse) to his contemporaries 'in order not to be stoned by them, if they suspected him of knowing that they don't exist.' Literature is intrinsically non-sociable; it is, so to speak, language without an address (and therefore diametrically opposed to the *Loisirs de la poste...*). The pressure behind nearly all Mallarmé's published work would then be reducible to a kind of prudence. Publication would be the gesture of self-protection which allows the writer to pursue literature, privately and secretly, elsewhere.

But we should perhaps be skeptical of any such downgrading of circumstantial writing. First of all, the position just outlined would be easier to accept if the distinctions were clearer in Mallarmé's career between the occasional works, or those responding to particular pressures, and works reflecting other (non-contingent) sorts of compositional pressures. But not only is almost all Mallarmé's writing occasional; there is also nothing perceptible in the quality of the writing itself which might help us to distinguish between the occasional work and the non-occasional work. It would be convenient, for example, if we could say that *Les Dieux antiques*, *Les Dons de fruits glacés* and even *La Dernière mode* were written as concessions to necessity or pleasure, and that this was not the case for, say, the essays grouped under the title *Quant au livre*, the *Tombeaux* poems, and the sonnets which begin *Quelle soie aux baumes de temps* and *Victorieusement fui le suicide beau*. For whatever literary virtues critics may now be inclined to find in such works as *La Dernière mode* or *Les Mots anglais*,[2] the writing in both these volumes is sufficiently different from the prose of the 1890 articles on theater to make us feel that the fashion articles and the chapters on philology carry the sign (the stigma?) of pressing circumstance whereas the pieces in *Crayonné au théâtre* – do not? Pieces which have established Mallarmé's importance in literary history are as occasional as his translations of Poe or of Mrs W. C. Elphinstone Hope's *The Star of the Fairies*.

The assumptions which govern the distinctions just made may sound foolish to us. We do not, after all, exclude the works written for particular occasions, or works which evoke specific circumstances in the writer's life, from the canon of great literature. Shakespeare's sonnets are as 'addressed' as Mallarmé's *Vers de circonstance*, and Milton's *Lycidas* and Keats's *Adonais* obviously owe their literary existence to highly particular circumstances. However, our tradition does include a certain suspicion of works in which a writer's response to personal or historical circumstances is not mediated by myth or sublimated into a universalized or abstract discourse. *Andromaque* and *Phèdre* are perhaps as revealing about social milieu as *Les Femmes savantes* and *Le Misanthrope*, but in order to appreciate this we must first of all demythify the tragic plot. And yet this also strips the work of its dignity: the priority of tragedy over comedy in classical esthetics is a function of the former's a-historical nature. The sign of the contingent in literature is a blackball in a hierarchical theory of literary *genres*.

Mallarmé, without having such a theory, frequently appears to be defending its values. He is always devaluing the circumstantial, while his work, far from being diminished or made impossible by circumstance, is actually sustained, as we shall see, by an extremely original relation to the contingent. I have referred to the autobiographical letter sent to Verlaine in 1885, in which Mallarmé not only relegates *Les Dieux antiques* and *Les Mots anglais* to the category of works explainable only by material need (we might not have them if Mallarmé didn't enjoy boating so much), but also speaks of all his published verse and poems in prose as having no other value than that of 'keeping his hand in.' And, adopting a distinction already used by Baudelaire, Mallarmé adds: '...quelque réussi que puisse être quelquefois un des [a word is missing] à eux tous, c'est bien juste s'ils composent un album, mais pas un livre' (*O.C.*, p. 663). The Book will be anonymous and noncircumstantial; it will, presumably, justify the scorn which Mallarmé expresses, in 'Le Mystère dans les lettres,' for those 'camelots' or 'street-hawkers,' who, 'activés par la pression de l'instant,' fail to spread 'le nuage, précieux, flottant sur l'intime gouffre de chaque pensée,' and therefore produce something 'common' ('vulgaire l'est ce à quoi on décerne, pas plus, un caractère immédiat' (*O.C.*, p. 384).[3] But if Mallarmé himself encourages us to believe that 'the pressure of the moment' will result in something esthetically mediocre, he also prevents us from making any such connection. The circumstantial is devalued, but how and against what are we to measure a body of circumstantial work which runs the gamut from the *Tombeaux* poems to the *Mots anglais*? We begin to suspect that the Mallarméan prejudice against circumstantiality is both strategic and dismissible. It pushes us into obsolete assumptions about the relation between contingency and value in art, while Mallarmé's work in fact forestalls any critical moves inspired by such assumptions.

Furthermore, the elitist perspective on literature as language without an address is by no means unambiguous in Mallarmé. It is true that throughout his career, from the 1862 essay 'L'Art pour tous' to the piece entitled 'Solitude' in *Divagations*), Mallarmé frequently reaffirms the apparently desirable divorce between the artist and the audience for art. In the early essay, 'art for everyone' is an 'esthetic heresy,' a heresy peculiar to the modern period, in which 'this impiety, the popularization of art,' has been furthered both by the teaching of literature in schools and the multiplication of inexpensive editions of literary works. In order to resist a scandalous inference of esthetic democracy from political democracy, Mallarmé insists that the artist 'must remain an aristocrat' (*O.C.*, pp. 259). Émilie Noulet has argued that Mallarmé will remain faithful to the esthetic elitism of this 1862 essay for the next thirty years.[4] But in fact 'L'Art pour tous' is a misleading juvenile manifesto; it provides a simplistic version of Mallarmé's feelings about the unprecedented diffusion of art in the modern period, and it gives no indication of Mallarmé's fascination with the possible use of art as a form of social conversion.

This fascination does not necessarily rule out the possibility of drawing a line between art and non-art. Rather, art as a mode of discourse would be subsumed within a more general concept of all discourse as *positioned address*. 'Toast funèbre' and 'Remémoration d'amis belges' are as much experiments in contingent, positioned discourse as, say, *La Dernière mode*. Indeed, if, in his autobiographical letter to Verlaine, Mallarmé writes that the issues he composed of *La Dernière mode* 'servent encore quand je les dévêts de leur poussière à me faire longtemps rêver' (*O.C.*, p. 664),[5] and if he thereby appears to exempt that journal from the category of works undertaken only because of financial need and which it would be best not to mention, it may be because *La Dernière mode* was the closest Mallarmé came to actually exercising some control over public taste.

The first issue of *La Dernière mode* deceptively suggests a more passive role for the journal: its principal object will be to help its women readers to find new sources of pleasure in contemporary art and fashion, and serious intellectual works will, it is promised, be discussed 'toujours selon le goût du jour [always according to contemporary fashion]' (*O.C.*, pp. 718 and 716). But *La Dernière mode* is a much more ambitiously active enterprise. It is an impressive guide to multitudinous aspects of modern urban life. The issues which Mallarmé single-handedly composed give advice on how to dress, what and where to eat, what theatrical events to attend, what books to read, what to pack for lunch if one is at the seashore or on a hunt, what exhibits to see and what bookstores to frequent, which railroad stations in Paris lead to which resorts, what books parents should buy for their children, how to make coconut jam or prepare a salve for chilblain, how to install a 'rich, exquisite, bizarre' mobile ceiling which, although one is 'condemned to the misfortune of a rented apartment,' will remind one's guests of a town house's 'beautiful coffered ceiling brought from the country' (*O.C.*, 770–1). In *La Dernière mode*, the 'orphic explanation of the Earth' has been transformed into a comprehensive *explication mondaine* of modern city life. And, in a sense, the journal is as impersonal as the Work was to have been. If we entertain doubts about Mallarmé's having become, as he announced to Cazalis in 1867, 'une aptitude qu'a l'univers spirituel à se voir à se développer à travers ce qui fut moi,' in *La Dernière mode* he perhaps did become an aptitude or medium through which the City might speak, a speaking appropriately disseminated among such *noms de plume* as Mme Marguerite de Ponty, Miss Satin, Zizi, 'bonne mulâtre de Surate' (who provided the recipe for coconut jam), and the anonymous 'teacher in one of the lycées in Paris' who has promised his 'enlightened aid' to Mme de Ponty in the section of the review devoted to educational books.

Mallarmé's interest in journalism was not as short-lived as *La Dernière mode*, only eight issues of which were published (from September to December, 1874). In 1887, for example, he contributed a series of articles on the theater to *La Revue indépendante*, and from February through November 1895, he wrote monthly pieces for *La Revue blanche*. It is characteristic of his unsettled sense of the conditions he wished to choose for his own writing that Mallarmé, in his first theatrical chronicles, should emphasize both how much he looks forward to not going to the theater and how little he expects to say in these articles. But we should probably not conclude from such remarks – nor from the passages which give priority to the book over the theater – that Mallarmé judges the written work to be superior to the theatrical spectacle. Rather, it seems clear from the chapters entitled 'Planches et feuillets' and 'Solennité' in the prose collection *Divagations*, that the 'book' which Mallarmé prefers to theater simultaneously replicates and annihilates theater. 'Quelle représentation! le monde y tient; un livre, dans notre main, s'il énonce quelque idée auguste, supplée à tous les théâtres, non par l'oubli qu'il en cause mais les rappelant impérieusement, au contraire' (*O.C.*, p. 334). And Mallarmé asks, in 'Planches et feuillets,' if the traditional writer of verse, 'celui qui s'en tient aux artifices humbles et sacrés de la parole,' is going to compete with Wagner. The answer is affirmative. The poet produces 'un opéra sans accompagnement ni chant, mais parlé; maintenant le livre essaiera de suffire, pour entr'ouvrir la scène intérieure et en chuchoter les échos. Un ensemble versifié convie à une idéale représentation...' (*O.C.*, p. 328). But this is only half the movement. If Mallarmé goes to the book in order to find theater, he will then return to the theater in order to realize the book. In 'Solennité,' Mallarmé refers to 'un esprit, réfugié au nombre de plusieurs feuillets, [qui] défie la civilisation négligeant de construire à son rêve, afin qu'elles aient lieu, la Salle prodigieuse et la Scène' (*O.C.*, p. 334).[6] There is an ideal-real stage yet to be built. And since the book appears to have served as a kind of de-realization of the spectacle, we might say that Mallarmé's theatrical goal is *de-realized theater realized*.

What would this mean, exactly? It may at first seem that a theater mediated by the book would be merely a more 'intellectual' or abstract theater. Mallarmé appears to be pointing in that direction when he speaks of the defiant intelligence just referred to as 'placed beyond circumstances' and as indifferent to the 'accompaniment' of actors and music to his mental theater, or when he approvingly notes 'this modern tendency' which consists of removing poetry from 'all contingencies of representation.' Theatrical contingency includes the physical presence of actors playing dramatic characters and, even more radically, the shaping of meaning in any narrativized fiction whatsoever. Poetic metaphor, unlike theater as we know it, 'simulates' and 'embodies' heroes 'juste dans ce qu'il faut apercevoir pour n'être pas gêné de leur présence, un trait' (*O.C.*, pp. 329 and 334).[7]

Mallarmé's reservations about Wagner have to do with the persistence of story, or legends, in a theater otherwise concerned with the pre-anecdotal initiations of human history. In the 'Rêverie d'un poète français' on Wagner, the latter is insistently praised as an artist of beginnings, until, having affirmed that not since Hellenic times has an audience had the privilege – offered by Wagner – of considering the secret of their origins ('le secret, réprésenté, d'origines') and having argued that in Wagner, music, simplified to its 'visée initiale,' (its original aims), generates the vitality of drama, Mallarmé unexpectedly reproaches Wagnerian beginnings for their remoteness from the source of all origins. 'Tout se retrempe au ruisseau primitif: pas jusqu'à la source. Si l'esprit français,' Mallarmé continues in what we recognize as an allusion to his own ambitions, 'strictement imaginatif et abstrait, donc poétique, jette un éclat, ce ne sera pas ainsi: il répugne, en cela d'accord avec l'Art dans son intégrité, qui est inventeur, à la Légende. Voyez-les, des jours abolis ne garder aucune anecdote énorme et fruste, comme une prescience de ce qu'elle apporterait d'anachronisme dans une représentation théâtrale, Sacre d'un des actes de la Civilisation.' (And, in a scornful footnote: 'Exposition, Transmission de Pouvoirs, etc., t'y vois-je, Brünnhild ou qu'y ferais-tu, Siegfried!') In the place of myths (happily 'dissolved' by nineteenth-century thought), Mallarmé proposes a single myth, 'dégagé de personnalité, car il compose notre aspect multiple ...un fait spirituel, l'épanouissement de symboles ou leur préparation,' a myth which would be a collective symbolization of 'nos rêves de sites ou de paradis,' and which would celebrate 'une réciprocité de preuves' exchanged between Man and 'son authentique séjour terrestre' (*O.C.*, pp. 543–5).[8]

The French poet's revery on Richard Wagner impressively evokes what would surely have been a curiously arid theatrical event. Stripped of story, of characters, of spectacle, of music, of all the occasions and contingencies of drama, Mallarmé's theater suggests a kind of unpleasant civic obligation, public re-celebrations of the founding of the City, of the Transmission of Powers...But such suggestions are also very vague, and this may be because Mallarmé was in fact more concerned with the occasion of theater than with the content of any recitation of the pre-primitive sources of the civic. In the passage from the Wagner essay which evokes a single myth so devoid of personality that, theatricalized, it would lead to 'quelque éclair suprême, d'où s'éveille la Figure que Nul n'est,' Mallarmé also comes close to identifying this 'spiritual fact' with the visual attention brought to it by an audience. A nameless mythical type needs, for its development, no place other than 'le fictif foyer de vision dardé par le regard d'une foule' (*O.C.*, p. 545).[9]

Furthermore, the fragments published by Scherer in *Le 'Livre' de Mallarmé* suggest that 'the orphic explanation of the Earth' became, in the course of Mallarmé's obsessive and fruitless plans for its realization, a question of logistics rather than truth, a model of performative positioning. The Master-text itself would apparently have been a sort of theatrical occasion. Mallarmé's notes deal much more elaborately with the circumstantial details of how the Book would be offered to an audience than with the nature of its message. Far from having an ideal ontological autonomy which would allow it to dispense with particular audiences, the 'spiritual universe' which was presumably to manifest itself through the dead Stéphane Mallarmé's anachronistic, directorial presence seems, in Mallarmé's thought, to have moved to a purely contingent space defined by an audience's attention. 'Each performance,' Mallarmé wrote, 'implies 24 pages, or 3 pages... × 8. (as many as there are guests who, without knowing it, represent the secret of the performance.' And: 'one proves something only with respect to others/to prove by reading.' Mallarmé even goes so far as to suggest that the Book is 'proven,' its value authenticated, by the fact that it is bought. As Scherer comments: 'The perfect congruity of the work and its audience is a sign of literature's existence. It is even, properly speaking, the definition of literature.'[10]

The recitation of the Book would have been a considerably sparer event than the ceremonies pointed to in Mallarmé's essay on Wagner. In both cases, however, the theater envisaged by Mallarmé is non-figurative, and in the case of the Book it would have been constituted by nothing more dramatic than a writer coming out to read in front of a group of people. It is by no means clear what might have been read at the performances of the Book, just as we have very little idea of what Mallarmé actually said at his legendary Tuesday-evening receptions at 87, rue de Rome. What he seems to have done with an undefinable brilliance during these evenings – and this is perhaps not irrelevant to the way Mallarmé planned for the Book's performance – was to position himself for receiving, and to solicit a touchingly devout attention for messages never delivered. But this was perhaps a great deal. That is, it was a modest yet decisive aspect in Mallarmé's re-definition of cultural expectations. Disciples came to the rue de Rome in order to justify their thinking of themselves as disciples; but they were treated as if that justification were to be found nowhere except in the sociability created by their mistaken notion that Mallarmé had something to say to them.

A particularly genial version of Mallarmé's readiness to produce art under 'the pressure of the moment' is given in the prose poem, 'La Déclaration foraine.' But the piece is also a particularly revealing instance of Mallarmé's extracting sense from circumstances by removing himself from them. As I noted a few pages back, he begins his notes on theater by announcing that he will stay away from theaters. Mallarmé's manner of attending (to) occasions consists in his leaving them. Persuaded by the woman with whom he is driving happily, and silently, through a suburban landscape to stop at a crowded fairground, the narrator of 'La Déclaration foraine' gallantly recites a poem for the crowd of people assembled around the table on which the woman has impulsively climbed and where she is imprudently promising a spectacle to a paying audience. The woman is doubly grateful: for the recitation which saved her from the crowd's disappointment, and for the poem itself – *Le chevelure vol d'une flamme à l'extrême* – which celebrates and publicizes the woman's hair as a flight of solar flame within the poet's desires. The intimate poem of desire is the result of a public pressure. It might never, as the woman points out afterwards, have been formulated in the 'conjoint isolation' of their carriage '... mais ceci jaillit, forcé, sous le coup de poing brutal à l'estomac, que cause une impatience de gens auxquels coûte que coûte et soudain il faut proclamer quelque chose fût-ce la rêverie...' (*O.C.*, p. 283).[11]

'Le Déclaration foraine' perversely suggests that silence is broken when the conditions of utterance have modified the motives for utterance, made them richly undecidable. Alone with the woman in the carriage, the poet feels no need to break the silence eulogized in the first paragraph. He speaks his desire only when his relation to its object is mediated by the crowd's impatience. Even more strikingly, it is only under the pressure of that impatience that the earlier references to the setting sun are revealed as already carrying the poet's excited awareness of the woman's hair. An abrupt change of occasion – the move from the silent carriage to the noisy fairground – leads the poet to articulate the sexualizing power of the 'bizarre and purple twilight' of the first, and lost, occasion. Everything is circumstantial, yet sense never *adheres* to circumstances. Occasions are abandoned so that their meanings may become visible. Recited desires refer to desires mediated neither by the formal rules of the Shakespearean sonnet nor by an audience of strangers; and it is as if the carriage had been left so that the reasons for not losing its privacy might be expressed. The exceptional courtesy with which Mallarmé's writing responds to the solicitations of particular occasions is, at the same time, an equally courteous refusal to concede that the interest of the response depends on a fixed attention to the occasion.

This displaced attentiveness is crucial for an understanding of Mallarméan difficulty. I have, in this study, been emphasizing Mallarmé's subversion of literary authority as a pre-condition for the play of circumstantial writing. And yet it is precisely the deprecating of that authority (and, more specifically, a certain de-poeticizing of language), as well as Mallarmé's extraordinary surrender to the contingent, which result in his most difficult writing. How should we define and respond to his obscurity?

From the perspective of the insistence in, for example, 'L'Art pour tous' on the aristocratic nature of art, and in the light of Mallarmé's proclaimed nostalgia in that essay for the 'gold clasps of old missals' and the 'sacred hieroglyphs of papyrus rolls' (*O.C.*, p. 257), obscurity can be thought of as the modern writer's defense against being read. Richard Poirier recently spoke of modernism as 'an attempt to perpetuate the power of literature as a privileged form of discourse. By its difficulty it tries, paradoxically, to reinvoke the connections, severed more or less by the growth of mass culture, between the artist and the audience.' This 'special connection' is now to be created by textual surfaces which defy any easy assumptions about the possibility of connectedness; a small community of readers is 'asked to participate in a shared text from which others are to be excluded.'[12]

But obscurity itself, as Mallarmé recognized with some exasperation, can become a popular fashion. 'De fait, on commence,' he notes in a piece on the theater first printed in the *National Observer* in June 1893, 'à l'endroit de ces suprêmes ou intactes aristocraties que nous gardions, littérature et arts, la feinte d'un besoin presque un culte: on se détourne, esthétiquement, des jeux intermédiaires proposés au gros du public, vers l'exception et tel moindre indice, chacun se voulant dire à portée de comprendre quoi que ce soit de rare' (*O.C.*, p. 325). Hermeticism becomes a rather desperate strategy, and in 'Solitude' we even have the writer calling back the journalist who has just asked him what he thinks of Punctuation in order to add to his remarks, 'par pudeur,' a little obscurity. *Any* public occasion could thus become an opportunity for ingenious dissembling, and 'Solitude' ends with an evocation of two men cordially hiding their thought from each other in conversation – 'reliquat des surannés combats d'esprit généreux et baroques ou conformément au monde dont les lettres sont le direct affinement – ... pour réserver leur intégrité' (*O.C.*, pp. 408–9).[13] The failure of communication is a function of the integrity of thought itself.

Obscurity in literature would therefore be both strategic and substantive. It is as if the writer, in order to protect the inherently arcane meanings of art from the violations of easy understanding and clarifying explications, superimposed a layer of tactical obscurity in order to prevent access to the more sacred core of intrinsic obscurity. But such tactics are of course ambiguous, and Mallarmé, like other difficult modern writers, certainly knew that the hermetic surfaces of his writing fascinated readers as much as they alienated them. Difficulty might be thought of as the principal element in the textual imperialism which I mentioned earlier in this study. It can function – it has functioned – as the justification, or pretext, for centralizing certain texts as inexhaustible objects of interpretation. We might, however, ask to what extent this centralization is the work of the most prestigious modernist texts themselves, and to what extent it expresses certain critical decisions *about* modernism. Poirier notes how little critical acknowledgement there has been that works such as *The Waste Land* and *Ulysses* 'are a sort of battleground: the flow of material wars against a technology which, however determined, is inadequate to the task of controlling the material.' Criticism has almost invariably treated these texts as if their difficulty could be resolved through exegesis; an anxious desire to perform 'some possibly terminal and encompassing acts of interpretation' has led to emphases on the substance rather than on the activity of allusiveness or schematization in modern writing. Poirier suggests that the difficulty – and the modernity – of writers as different from one another as Mallarmé, Yeats, Joyce, Faulkner and Pynchon lie less in their elaborate 'formal placements,' the learning, the cultural displays, the mechanics of structuring which their works exhibit, than in 'the act of *dis*placement by which one form is relinquished for another.' The formal and allusive puzzles which have fascinated and immobilized criticism are most interesting not for what they 'mean,' but rather as signs of 'the enormous difficulty of mastering a technology,' of the 'inadequacy of forms and structures or styles to the life they propose to explain or include.'[14]

It is of course true that the writers just mentioned partly encourage the strenuous exegeses which treat their works as puzzles to be solved. Mallarmé's orphic allusions to an orphic explanation of the Earth, Yeats' system, Eliot's Notes, and Faulkner's Christian symbolism all encourage criticism to forget the revealed inadequacy of all explanations in these writers and to treat local, temporary acts of usually intricate shaping as definitive statements. Nevertheless, as Poirier persuasively argues, modernist texts also offer the model of a very different type of interpretive activity. The continuous relinquishing of forms in these texts is the consequence of the writer's continuous interpretation of his own forms. For his own reading of those forms immediately replaces them, may even expose their factitiousness. Or, to put this in other terms, the meaning of modernist texts would *be* 'their capacity to mean different things;' it would reside 'in the performance...of reading in the act of writing,' in the writer's readiness to monitor and to dismiss acts of signification, a readiness at least as great, and in a sense more moving, than the culturally anxious need to shape such acts.[15]

In the heroine of *The Golden Bowl*, James gives us a novelistic emblem of the power of difficulty in art. In the second half of the novel, Maggie Verver is treated like an impenetrable work of art; everyone around her is reduced to frantic conjectures about her enigmatic, withheld sense. Interpretations multiply, compete, and mostly disappear around her silent, statue-like presence. *The Golden Bowl* is about the coercive power of certain forms; more specifically, it deals with the resistance of formal arrangements to the interpretive scramble to discover definitive meanings in those arrangements. What Maggie 'means' – and what characters as excessively and obtusely intelligent as Fanny Assingham and Charlotte Verver fail to see – is indistinguishable from the move by which she has made herself the object of the others' attention. She is a model of positioned rather than of substantive sense; the 'message' which she has for the others is exactly identical to, and goes no further than, the self-displacements by which she has become, finally, an object of their attention.

It is true that, somewhat like the modernist texts alluded to a moment ago, Maggie herself is in part responsible for the type of power which she acquires. Her imperialistic control over the other figures in the novel is, most directly, the result of their mistaken belief that they can possess her sense; they are victimized by their own yearnings for settled interpretations. And yet, if Maggie 'means' nothing, her moves are also consciously designed to move the others back into certain fixed postures. That is, her own displacements are at once an exercise in the shifting artfulness of self-displacement itself, and a strategy meant to re-locate the others in a strict and fixed observation of inherited social forms and institutions. She (and, through her, James) vacillates between a view of art best represented in the novel by her father (a view in which forms are collected, centralized and immobilized in museums), and a notion of art as improvised, even aleatory 'mobile syntheses.'[16] These different views closely parallel the ambiguous status of sexual passion in *The Golden*

Bowl. Sex is shaped and 'covered over' by the given forms and obligations of marriage, but it also breaks loose of any institutional definitions whatsoever and isolates Maggie in an 'improvised "post"' which, James notes, would be marked on a map of social relations only by the geography of 'the fundamental passions.'[17] Seen as a work of art, Maggie naturally offers a sublimated version of this alternative, and in esthetic terms the parallel to uncharted sexual desire would, I think, be a mobilizing of forms which makes them radically, permanently unreadable. And this unreadability would be a function not of mystifyingly intricate surfaces beyond which lie graspable meanings, but rather of sense performatively dissolved in the time of the work and perhaps even demanding, correlatively, self-dissolving interpretations....

On the basis of these observations, one might distinguish between two types of difficulty in modern writing, although the distinction, as I have suggested, perhaps applies most forcefully to critical moves both toward and within modernist texts. On the one hand, difficulty has nourished textual imperialism when it has resulted in the interpretive centering of highly valued texts, a centering which reinforces traditional cultural hierarchies and privileges. On the other hand, difficulty can be created by (and critically treated as) an extreme mobility of attention, a continuous moving away from what might be called the narrative ordering of thought. The former type of difficulty demands exegesis (which is itself a narrativizing activity of the mind), and it therefore implicitly asserts the epistemological priority of sense which *can* be narrativized over interpretive play; the latter type of difficulty largely precludes exegesis. The former, finally, is consistent with the metaphysical seriousness of a Book which would 'explain' the universe, while the latter may be the product not only of a continuous relinquishing of tentative formal arrangements but also of a playfully promiscuous attention always ready to swerve to the side of its objects and to wander in a variety of sensually appealing digressive activities.

In the case of Mallarmé, the difficulty of his work should be thought of not as being in contradiction with its contingency, but rather as a function of that contingency. It could even be said that obscurity in Mallarmé's writing is frequently a mode of his sociability; it *is* the special way in which he makes himself available to circumstances. But in order to understand Mallarmé's relation to the contingent, we should first of all look at his most radical effort to suppress all contingency: *Igitur ou La Folie d'Elbehnon.* I spoke in Chapter One of the annihilating movements of thought, and, in my discussion of *Hérodiade*, I distinguished between the productively mistaken replications of objects by consciousness, and the narcissistic effort to substitute for these non-mimetic replications a perfect identity between thought and its objects. In *Igitur*, Mallarmé stages an even more radical temptation: that of suppressing any consciousness *of* (the world or the self) as the precondition for a suicidal, non-articulated 'gathering-in' of the mind – or in other terms, for a divorce of consciousness from all existential circumstance.

The extraordinary strangeness of *Igitur* has to do with its undecidable ideality. It is an explicitly, insistently scrupulous and methodical 'reduction' of all those references to the outside which, paradoxically, constitute the activity of a pure, objectless consciousness. Igitur's mind is crowded with signs of existence external to it: the beating of wings, paneled walls, tombs, corridors, a spider's web, furnishings in a room. The crucial second section of the tale, a section of which we have several versions, records Igitur's attempt to guarantee the unreality of all these references. In an intricate parody of Descartes' intuition of existence (his own, that of the world, that of God) from a movement of radical doubt, the Mallarméan narrator repeatedly proclaims the elimination of doubt in order to assert the reduction of all space and time to empty self-reflection. For all its abstractions, *Igitur* is surprisingly dramatic, and the drama is generated by an attentiveness at once nervous and almost madly patient to all the visions, sounds, and movements which *might* have existed as something more than tokens of a moving away from all existence. Thus, at the beginning of Chapter II, the narrator speaks of 'une motion [qui] dure, marquée plus pressante par un double heurt, qui n'atteint plus ou pas encore sa notion'; and, later on in the same section, the lingering 'vision of a place' is proclaimed to be nothing more than the 'reminiscence of a lie,' for 'la symétrie parfaite des déductions prévues démentait' the reality of the place. But the perfect certainty of a successfully achieved self-consciousness – 'la conscience de soi' – *is* a mind emptily 'occupied.' The symmetrical deductions which abolish all real places are simultaneously 'places' and logical movements. In the passage substantiating the certainty just referred to, the distinctions which thought might make between abstract and concrete are rendered obsolete by the operations of thought itself. But language can express the obsoleteness of distinctions which support its structures only by feigning, as it were, an ignorance of its own resistance to the blurring of ontological boundaries. Thus the logical inconceivability

of thought as a mode of exteriority is masked by a normalizing but
wholly strange syntactical congruence of outside and inside:

Cette fois, plus nul doute; la certitude se mire en l'évidence: en vain,
réminiscence d'un mensonge, dont elle était la conséquence, la vision d'un
lieu apparaissait-elle encore, telle que devait être, par exemple, l'intervalle
attendu, ayant, en effet, pour parois latérales l'opposition double des
panneaux, et pour vis-à-vis, devant et derrière, l'ouverture de doute nul
répercutée par le prolongement du bruit des panneaux, où s'enfuit le
plumage, et dédoublée par l'équivoque exploré, la symétrie parfaite des
déductions prévues démentait sa réalité; il n'y avait pas à s'y tromper c'était
la conscience de soi (à laquelle l'absurde même devait servir de lieu) – sa
réussite. (*O.C.*, pp. 437–8)[18]

But in *Igitur*, and for Igitur, this is not enough. The movement
of mind by which the thinking subject snaps away from, and
annihilates, its real setting can be taken not only as proof of the power
of consciousness, but also as a sign of the repellently contingent
heterogeneity of its contents. The night-filled room in which Igitur
is present as a still-perceptible shadow is analogous to the relation
between consciousness as total night and the forms of thought which
stand out in their shadowy brightness against that night. The
productivity of mind becomes an obstacle to the mind's power to
annihilate; or, more exactly, mind annihilates *by* multiplying forms.
Thus a distinction appears in *Igitur* between consciousness and
nothingness. In one version of Chapter II, the shadow, 'gênée de la
certitude parfaite de soi,' tries to escape from that certainty, 'et de
rentrer en elle, en son opacité.' Just before this passage, the place
of perfect certainty is described as containing myriad shadows on its
two sides and, on the sides of those shadows, 'dans les parois
opposées, qui se réfléchissaient, deux trouées d'ombre massive qui
devait être nécessairement l'inverse de ces ombres, non leur apparition, mais leur disparition, ombre négative d'eux-mêmes' (*O.C.*,
p. 446).[19] The perfect certainty of consciousness is represented as
shadows which are negative versions of other shadows; the former
enact the disappearance of the latter. The narrator retraces Igitur's
discovery of figures for the disappearance of all figures; but the very
figuration of negativity comes to be perceived as blocking its
realization.

As in *Hérodiade*, consciousness is at once darkness and light (the
'pure shadows' in the place of perfect certainty carry 'le volume de
leurs destinées, et la pure clarté de leur conscience [the volume of their
destinies, and the pure clarity of their consciousness]'), but now –
wholly internalized, dissociated from a princess's glittering physical

beauty – the light is troubling evidence of consciousness *as* articulated evidence. This evidence is, interestingly, associated with a sign of Igitur's physical life, the sound of his heart: the illuminated triumph of Igitur's consciousness is hopelessly connected to a particular, and particularizing existence. Thus, in the definitive version of Chapter II, Igitur seeks to escape from the light of a biologically and historically conditioned consciousness into a Shadow prior to any conditions whatsoever:

Je n'aime pas ce bruit [the beating of his heart]: cette perfection de ma certitude me gêne: tout est trop clair, la clarté montre le désir d'une évasion; tout est trop luisant, j'aimerais rentrer en mon Ombre incréée et antérieure, et dépouiller par la pensée le travestissement que m'a imposé la nécessité, d'habiter le cœur de cette race (que j'entends battre ici) seul reste d'ambiguïté. (*O.C.*, p. 438)[20]

The self-reflective consciousness, through which Igitur aspires to escape from the contingencies of an historical self, is, then, uncomfortably like a powerful self-affirmation. The timeless stillness of absolutely specularized thought has, perhaps unexpectedly, provided the material for a narrative rendering of the 'figures of thought' in which Igitur perceives the process of self-specularization. And the very certainty which those figures provide reconstitute Igitur as an historical will. Thus the curious anti-dualistic doubling of Mallarmé's hero: in order to avoid the separations of consciousness from itself inherent in reflexive acts of consciousness, separations which provide the material for this literary tale and therefore record and publicize Igitur's unique place in the history of his race, Igitur posits himself as 'uncreated and anterior Shadow,' as 'un personnage dont la pensée n'a pas conscience de lui-même,... dernière figure, séparée de son personnage par une fraise arachnéenne et qui ne se connaît pas: aussi, maintenant que sa dualité est à jamais séparée, et que je n'ouïs même plus à travers lui le bruit de son progrès, je vais m'oublier à travers lui, et me dissoudre en moi' (*O.C.*, p. 439).[21]

But even here, in what appears to be a sliding into undifferentiated darkness, or formless neutrality, Igitur continues to conceive this final immobilizing movement as access to another *self*. Even the 'Ombre incréée et antérieure' is *his* shadow, and the opacity meant to save Igitur from perfect self-certainty is perhaps still a 'self-belonging' consciousness even if it is no longer a consciousness *of* self. As Blanchot has written, a living thought – the 'I' of Igitur – always supports the nothingness which it claimed to evoke. Mallarmé's metaphysical tale is also an energetically guided personal narrative; it is dominated, not by that powerless but incessant murmuring of a voiceless voice, of what Blanchot calls 'le néant comme être, le désœuvrement de l'être [nothingness as being, the idleness of being],' but rather by the forceful deductions, recapitulations and conjunctions... of the aristocratic Igitur.[22]

Mallarmé's philosophical tale analyzes a process of aggravated negativity. Consciousness first of all erases the objects of perception. But consciousness also separates itself from its own representations. The subject-object duality disappears in order to be replaced by a paradoxical specular duality: what Igitur calls 'perfect certainty' appears to be the effect of a separation of consciousness from itself which produces only an empty awareness or reflection of the representations of consciousness. Each of these distancing movements is a kind of negation: images negate objects, and a consciousness *of* the mind's images implies a consciousness sufficiently depleted of those images to see them as objects. Finally, what Igitur calls his own opacity is reached when the originating term of a movement is both annihilated and neither replaced nor reflected; this is the still emptiness of an objectless, 'pointless' consciousness. But if, to repeat Blanchot's comment, a 'living thought' continues to support this radical experience of consciousness as non-thought, the only 'abstraction' left is biological death. In *Igitur*, the hero's suicide is the ultimate refinement of the mind, the existential act which purifies consciousness of existence.

Igitur develops a simple proposition: consciousness is narcissistic and suicidal because it is constitutionally negativizing. Mallarmé both glamorizes and demystifies the culturally fascinating image of the solitary, profound, concentrated thinker. He suggests that the teleology of consciousness is its own destruction. For while human life would be inconceivable without the abstracting power of mind, the exercise of that power inexorably works toward the hypostatizing of negativity. The objects of thought are wasted by thought (annihilated; treated like waste); but, as *Igitur* suggests, the full power of thought is experienced only if the wasting movement can be severed from its objects. The infatuation of thought with its own negativizing power would lead, ideally, to the climactic yet indefinite satisfaction of an infinitely repeated dying. Arrested attention thus initiates the infinitely seductive experience of the destructiveness of consciousness. And, if Igitur's suicide is a *pis aller*, it may nonetheless be the only empirically conceivable alternative to a timeless dying.

There is, then, a power of consciousness wholly distinct from the human capacity to change the physical world. The power I refer to lies in an anti-vital, perhaps even anti-evolutionary capacity to make us love death, to make us see dying as power. Next to this version of the solitary thinker's desires, the more celebrated Faustian version may even seem somewhat superficial. More precisely, the Faustian image is undoubtedly more celebrated because it obscures the inherent or structural danger of consciousness by a sentimental complaint about the distance between thought and the world. Goethe's Faust, for example, disguises the threat which thought poses to life by presenting the abstracting nature of thought as a sign of its weakness (mind has not brought him close to Nature's secrets), whereas the movement of abstraction is in itself an invicible act of devastation. The Faustian myth obscures the nature of mind's destructiveness in a dramatic complaint about thought's technological weakness. It therefore sustains precisely that image of thought as sublimely ineffectual which *Igitur* demystifies.

Mallarmé's tale points to a necessarily hidden truth: human consciousness moves thanks to the biologically dysfunctional appeal of negativity. Igitur's adventure is in line with a highly valued philosophical tradition: the production of truth through the mental concentration of a solitary thinker. But Igitur's fate suggests that the cultural fascination with the image of the solitary, sublimating philosopher may be a way of legitimizing cultural destructiveness, and of ennobling the melancholy induced by cultural programs of renunciation. The menace which human thought poses to the world is not the result of a Faustian over-reaching of thought; it rather lies in an inclination, on the part of consciousness, to abandon the world for the sake of a possibly self-shattering and yet also self-authenticating spasm of negativity. The cultural dignity accorded to the abstractions of concentrated thought must be deconstructed, and understood as manifestations of the sensuality peculiar to suicidal desire.

In the January 1887 issue of *La Revue indépendante*, Mallarmé published the following poems under the title 'Sonnets I, II, III:'

I

Tout Orgueil fume-t-il du soir,
Torche dans un branle étouffée
Sans que l'immortelle bouffée
Ne puisse à l'abandon surseoir!

La chambre ancienne de l'hoir

De maint riche mais chu trophée
Ne serait pas même chauffée
S'il survenait par le couloir.

Affres du passé nécessaires
Agrippant comme avec des serres
Le sépulcre de désaveu,

Sous un marbre lourd qu'elle isole
Ne s'allume pas d'autre feu
Que la fulgurante console.

II

Surgi de la croupe et du bond
D'une verrerie éphémère
Sans fleurir la veillée amère
Le col ignoré s'interrompt.

Je crois bien que deux bouches n'ont
Bu, ni son amant ni ma mère,
Jamais à la même Chimère,
Moi, sylphe de ce froid plafond!

Le pur vase d'aucun breuvage
Que l'inexhaustible veuvage
Agonise mais ne consent,

Naïf baiser des plus funèbres!
A rien expirer annonçant
Une rose dans les ténèbres.

III

Une dentelle s'abolit
Dans le doute du Jeu suprême
A n'entr'ouvrir comme un blasphème
Qu'absence éternelle de lit.

Cet unanime blanc conflit
D'une guirlande avec la même,
Enfui contre la vitre blême
Flotte plus qu'il n'ensevelit.

Mais, chez qui du rêve se dore
Tristement dort une mandore
Au creux néant musicien

Telle que vers quelque fenêtre
Selon nul ventre que le sien,
Filial on aurait pu naître.[23]

These three pieces belong together. On the simplest narrative level, there is a temporal progression from the evening mentioned in the first line of the first poem, to the night evoked (by the 'ténèbres' of the final line) in the second poem, and finally to the dawn suggested by the uncertain light on the 'vitre blême' of the third sonnet. Also, the three pieces appear to be variations on the theme of absence. We have, as Émilie Noulet has noted, the house without pride or warmth, then the vase without flowers, and finally the bedroom without a bed.[24] But repetition is also modulation: from the rather heavy and stately mood of despondency in the first piece to the discreet, qualified suggestion in the 'Dentelle' poem that absence might have become presence, that a birth might have taken place.

In both *Igitur* and the sonnets of the triptych, Mallarmé asks us to consider the kind of attention which a solitary figure gives to the objects in a room. The problematic nature of that attention is more explicit in *Igitur* than in the sonnets: the hero of the earlier work continuously affirms the non-existence of what he 'sees,' and he is both comforted and disturbed by his successful abolishing of real places. In the triptych, the distinction between physical presence and physical absence seems clearer. It is not a question of verifying the ideality of 'objects,' their status as figures for 'la conscience de soi.' Rather, certain objects clearly in the room are mentioned, in the sonnets, as a kind of foil to other absent objects. 'La fulgurante console' points up the absence of any other light or fire in the room; the vase is mentioned only to draw our attention to the fact that it is empty; and the lace curtain opens onto an 'eternal absence' of a bed.

We could, however, also say the reverse: the absence of a fire, of a rose, and of a bed is the occasion for the poet's noting or producing certain kinds of presence. The simple dichotomy between presence and absence is undermined by the very terms which set up that dichotomy. This is particularly striking in the first poem which, by Mallarméan standards, is a rather stark and occasionally prosaic statement of absence. The second stanza of that poem, for example, is surprisingly flat. The dejected mood induced by the interrogative exclamation about Pride turning so quickly to smoke controls the perception of the room, makes for an obsessive but dimmed pre-occupation with the lack of heat, and explains the melancholy vision of the console as a tomb. But the last three stanzas do much more than repeat, through the metaphorical description of the unheated room, the inaugural meditation on extinguished pride. Absence and extinction take on a variety of forms in the poem: the smothered torch of Pride and the room without heat, but also the past evoked by the heir's ancient room as well as by his fallen trophies, the absence of the heir himself, and the extinction or denial of life by the 'sépulcre de désaveu,' the marble slab on the console table. Each version of absence both replicates and 'extinguishes' another version, and the poetic meditation on absence at once confirms and discredits the idea which it presumably develops. The theme of transitory hope and extinguished aspirations is itself extinguished in the proliferative power of its illustration. The consciousness of loss produces supplements to the loss which it describes and enacts.

The general subject of the sonnets is the relation between negativity and birth. This mysterious relation is somewhat prudently tested in the first poem through the various types of verbal resourcefulness in the poet's despondent evocations of loss and death: the archaic vocabulary ('un branle,' 'surseoir à,' and especially 'La chambre ancienne de l'*hoir*/De *maint* riche mais *chu* trophée') which, so to speak, re-surfaces in language in order to announce the extinctions of honors and ambitions from another age; the circumlocution 'sépulcre de désaveu' for the tomb-like marble slab; and the ambiguous construction of the first verse.[25] There is, above all, the unexpected word 'fulgurante' in the last verse of the sonnet. The dim lights, the absence of heat, the loss of all moral and physical *éclat* are not denied or made up for by this bizarrely bright console-table. (Etymologically, the brightness is that of a flash of lightning: 'fulgurant' derives from the Latin 'fulgor,' lightning.) Indeed, we must even try to think of the flashing splendor of the console-table as the confirmation of darkness and cold: 'no other fire burns than' the console-table. To look at that piece of furniture is to see a tomb confirming the absence of life and of warmth in the room; but to name it is to make an enigma of the statement in which it is named. In both cases, consciousness moves away from, abolishes an object; but the indescribable relation between the console-table as 'fulgurante' and the console-table as a cold tomb also shows that the possibility of losing sense is inherent in the act of creating sense. I do not mean that the tercets are senseless; rather, it is as if sense were detached from enunciation, were wandering in the intervals between different sense-making moves.

We have a similar dislodging of sense in the second sonnet. The

vase seems condemned to an 'inexhaustible veuvage.' Its androgynous shape will, we are told, remain unexploited: the vase is at once
an empty vessel and a 'col ignoré.' Nothing is poured into the vase,
and its neck appears even to refuse to penetrate the air surrounding
it; it will never 'exhale' or give birth to a rose. But while the sylph
thus asserts that no sexual union either has taken place or will take
place, the poem is enclosed, enfolded, by verbal realizations of erotic
energy and fulness. The astonishing first line – 'Surgi de la croupe
et du bond' – performs the sexual thrust which the rest of the poem
will deny. The very strangeness of a vigorous rising up from a leap
and a rump makes the phallic neck's movement more memorable,
more resistant to the subsequent interruption of that movement, as
well as to the vase's own refusal to breathe the promise of a flower
into the darkness. But even this refusal is gently circumvented by the
privileged position of 'une rose dans les ténèbres.' The poem realizes
what the vase fails to announce; a refusal is annuled by the richly
evocative visibility of the absent rose in the sonnet's final verse.

The triptych performs the annuling movement of consciousness *as
a procreative act*. The poems are a gradual vindication of the final
sonnet's climactic word: 'naître.' A powerful narrative logic leads
us to that word, at the same time that Mallarmé demonstrates how
unsuitable any narrative clarities whatsoever are to the birth-death
performed in these poems. The preoccupation with sexual union and
birth which begins in the second sonnet is initiated by the
supplementary assertiveness of the first sonnet. The proliferative
power with which the theme of absence is illustrated gives birth to
an ambiguous linguistic presence. More generally, we might say that
birth is always a supplement to the dying inherent in consciousness. The
presence to which that dying gives birth is, however, never 'full'; it
is an already de-realized presence by virtue of its having been
constituted by a movement of dying. In the triptych, this means that
linguistic assertiveness does not reinstate the fallen trophies and
extinguished pride of the first sonnet, nor does it cancel out, in the
second sonnet, the vase's wilful barrenness. Rather, the power of
language's supplemental creations is indistinguishable from the
powerlessness of particular words to enclose and to immobilize sense.

The sense of Mallarmé's poems is neither presence nor absence;
nor is it a 'compromise' between presence and absence. Rather, it
is the irreducible ambiguity of, for example, sexuality simultaneously
annuled and asserted, or the fiery radiance of a cold, tomblike table.
Language, Blanchot has written, creates enigmas rather than solves
them.[26] The assertively negativizing force of language inevitably

ruins hypothetically clear sense-making intentions. Literature is *naturally obscure*; 'transparent' writing can only be the result of a strenuous violation of language's tendency to displace rather than to immobilize sense. Linguistic practice unglues meaning from linguistic units. The sense established by words always slips into the intervals between words, and intervallic sense is that continuously disappearing presence which, in Mallarmé's writing, is made visible in an unprecedented manner.

Nothing could be more different from the accented slippage of the triptych than the specularizing strategies of the 'Ouverture ancienne' to *Hérodiade*, and of *Igitur*. It is as if, in these latter works, Mallarmé were trying to eliminate the supplemental effects of negativity, to impose a purely repetitive time on consciousness by entrapping language within symmetrical patterns. The lexical mirrors which I spoke of in *Hérodiade* (and which we also find in *Igitur*) can now be understood as verbal strategies designed to make each move of consciousness *only* the negativizing reflection of previous moves. Igitur seeks to sever the dying of consciousness from its procreative consequences. He would sink into his own opacity, and he finally hypostatizes negativity in a personal suicide. Igitur reduces the sensual appeal of consciousness to its power to initiate, ceaselessly, a process of dying. In the triptych, on the other hand, the sensualizing power of negativity is identical to its supplemental, or procreative power. The sexual suggestiveness of the second and third sonnets is co-extensive with the displacing of meanings; it is perhaps even an effect of the shattering of semantic locatability.

Sensuality in the triptych moves explicitly toward reproductive sexuality, although it is of course important to note that the birth retrospectively and hypothetically announced in the 'Dentelle' poem would have taken place 'selon nul ventre que' that of the person 'qui du rêve se dore.' Sexual union is not implied by the possibility of birth; the bed's absence is eternal, and nothing asks us to question the sylph's belief that neither his mother nor her lover has ever 'bu à la même Chimère.' The final poem in the triptych would seem to bring us back to the specularizing intentions of *Hérodiade*. The sound repetitions in verses 9 and 10 and the description of the room as the 'blanc conflit/D'une guirlande avec la même' reinforce the suggestion of a purely solipsistic creation. The only relation which the triptych appears to allow for is one of sameness. Apparently, the mandolin does not even give birth to something new; it is as if only the dreamer himself might have been born from the hollow musical nothingness of the instrument already sleeping within him.

But the triptych has, I believe, already invited us to consider this bizarrely sterile birth as a kind of self-differentiating solipsism. The final poem is as rich as the other two in mobile supplementarity. Rather than try to determine what situation is being referred to in the first stanza, for example, we might note how the sense of that stanza moves between the unqualified negativity of 's'abolit' and 'absence eternelle,' and the unsettled, even frivolously unsettled negativity of 'le doute du Jeu suprême.' Is the supreme Play what is not taking place on the absent bed behind the partly drawn curtain, or is it the mental activity which abolishes a curtain? Is the play on the (about-to-be) negated bed the object of doubt, or is the lace curtain abolished in the doubt inherent in a supreme Play of the mind? The poem takes place in the intervals between such alternatives of sense. Or, even more interestingly, the sonnet suggests – and this is its inescapable referentiality – that to look at the objects in a room is always to initiate the beneficent doubts of insecure perception and mobile thought.

The possibility of a solipsistic birth seems both to compensate for the missing sexual union perhaps evoked by stanza one, and to pick up the procreative clue in the floating, pregnant whiteness of stanza two. Self-repetition in the poem is, however, also self-differentiation. To a certain extent, exact temporal and spatial repetitions seem always to have enjoyed the status of epistemological or ontological 'proof' for Mallarmé. I'm thinking of Hérodiade's narcissism, of Igitur's striving toward the perfect certainty of 'la conscience de soi,' and, more generally, of the Mallarméan notion of sentences and thoughts adjusting their rhythm to the objects they purport to describe and thereby reproducing 'the attitude of that object,' or its 'position' in the world.[27] Literature 'proves' the world by authentically replicating it. The play of supplemental sense in the poems of the triptych suggests something quite different: a self-repetition which would be non-specular. In the final sonnet, the propagation of difference within and even by repetition is the result of both an erotics and an esthetic. An eroticized perception shatters perceptual logic. The sexual energy both aroused and thwarted by the bed's absence, for example, may determine the fertilizing if somewhat incoherent mobility of perception in stanza two. An omnipresent whiteness, instead of signifying merely absence or the 'burying' ('l'ensevelissement') of all objects of vision, is mobilized, and problematized, as conflict, as flight, and as floating. And the differential movements of an eroticized perception *may already be art*. For in that movement the biographical self we know as Stéphane

Mallarmé dies, and the depersonalized speaker of the work of art is born.

The myth of personality, as we saw in Chapter 1, explodes under the pressure of concentrated subjectivity. An erotically charged vision has the same mobilizing and scattering effect as the vibration produced by stiffened nerves, a vibration which, in the terms of Mallarmé's May 17, 1867 letter to Lefébure, transforms a purely cerebral thought into an impression. The triptych begins by mourning the loss of a grand historical self, but by the end of the third poem we should be able to see that the subject of the entire sequence has been the birth of a writer in and as the supplemental energies and the supplemental intervals of a negativizing thought. Only the voice of the second sonnet is identified, and our attention is dramatically drawn to the shift from a psychological and historical being to a creature of the lightest esthetic fancy – a creature whose problematic parents have perhaps never touched each other – by the placing, in the exact middle of the triptych, of a verse in which 'Moi' is equated with nothing more substantial, nothing more honored or capable of Pride, than the mildly, tentatively assertive ('Je crois bien que...') 'sylphe de ce froid plafond.' The triptych is an exemplary esthetic space in that it both displays and renders unfathomable the formative or ordering powers of art. The sonnets are a model of thematic repetition, at the same time that repetition annihilates theme. And this annihilating replication produces a presence radically different from a person, an intervallic presence which implicitly defines the esthetic as a repudiation of form, or, more accurately, as an enigmatic equivalence between formal elaborations and a continuous slippage of significance away from any locatable forms.

'One might have been born' from the mandolin's 'creux néant musicien' in the uncertain light of an imminent dawn. The negativity which nourishes art is perhaps a *suspended negativity*. The half-light of a new day creates a fruitful doubt about the identity and the place of objects, and perhaps therefore interrupts the movement of consciousness which would appropriate and abolish objects. It is as if the annihilating thinking of objects took place here without being completed. As a result, the uncertainties of thought stimulate the (mistakenly) replicative representations of the world which sustain art. Because Igitur's perfect certainty about the world's having been abolished by a completed thought makes the play of art superfluous, the only *jouissance* available to Mallarmé's triumphantly speculative hero is the suicidal pleasure of a pure, objectless, and final negativity. (It is part of the extraordinary, and the extraordinarily light, power

of the triptych that the sonnet closest, atmospherically, to *Igitur –
Tout Orgueil fume-t-il du soir...* – actually initiates the supplementarity, the propagation of sense from negativity which the tercets of
the final sonnet represent as a gestation from the hollow nothingness
of art.) The triptych is, so to speak, fertilized by a doubtful negativity
finally made explicit in the 'Dentelle' poem. A by no means negligible
result of this is Mallarmé's realism. We are, astonishingly, referred
to the external world by the very movement of consciousness which
negates it.

*Mallarmé moves away from his thought's negativizing power to move
away from the world.* The triptych performs an irony about the irony
intrinsic to consciousness. It partly dismisses its own repeated
dismissals. Consciousness always represents the world ironically, in
the sense that its representations of the world cannot help but have
a significance at odds with what they refer to. The expressed
consciousness of objects necessarily increases our distance from
objects. The ultimate logic of the ironic negativity of thought is
spelled out in *Igitur*. But Mallarmé goes further than *Igitur* – which
is of course also to say that he refuses to go that far. He is finely ironic
about negativity, and this supplemental fold of consciousness has the
odd and important effect of reaffirming the world's presence. And
since, as the triptych suggests, that reaffirmation can only stimulate
an appetitive, erotic curiosity, we might say that Mallarmé's ironic
treatment of negativity is a particularly civilized and an especially
sociable sign of human desire.

The sonnets of the triptych, unlike 'Toast funèbre,' 'Remémoration
d'amis belges,' and the 'Eventail de Madame Mallarmé,' are not
occasional poems. In one sense, they are extremely abstract poems:
they are 'about' the negativizing force of consciousness, and the
relation between absence or infertility and the birth of art. But,
characteristically, these subjects are contingent upon, are born from
a specific *location*. Philosophical reflection is physically positioned.
But the very category of philosophical poetry is rendered problematic
by virtue of the fact that there is no locatable thought in the sonnets.
An ontology of thought is performed entirely through a narrative of
perception. The radically non-Cartesian Mallarméan thinker alone
in a room does nothing but look at the objects in the room. His doubt,
far from being a deliberate tactical move designed to test the reality
of the self and of the world, is the very movement of his belief in the
world's reality. In Mallarmé, the abstracting movements of consciousness are not moves of transcendence; rather, they are exactly

identical to an ardent adherence to particular aspects of the world.

What does it mean to be present? The aberration of the 'interregnum' is its belief in the present. '...There is no Present, no,' Mallarmé informs his contemporaries in the essay 'L'Action restreinte,' ' – a present does not exist....' As we might expect, this assertion is ambiguous: does Mallarmé mean that there is never any present, that the present is a false concept, or does he simply mean, as he writes in the same piece, that his period is an historical tunnel, in which poetry can only be tried 'en de chastes crises isolément, pendant l'autre gestation en train' (*O.C.*, p. 372)? I have of course been arguing against any reading of Mallarmé which would emphasize his own teleological reading of this absence of a present. Everything, according to this interpretation, exists in order to be explained, summarized, concluded in the Book. But Mallarmé's writing works against any such belief; it continuously draws our attention to the slippage, inherent in human consciousness, away from any fully realized presence (including that of the present...). The error which Mallarmé attributes to his period is not an historical illusion; it is ontologically pathogenic. 'Voilà ce que, précisément, exige un moderne: se mirer, quelconque...' (*O.C.*, p. 375).[28] Mallarmé explains his contemporaries' taste for novels by their wish to recognize themselves in the stories they read; even 'the need to act' confessed to by the friend whom Mallarmé intermittently addresses in 'L'Action restreinte,' could be thought of as a need to see oneself unambiguously reflected in events. Hérodiade's narcissism, her desire to be fully present to herself, is re-enacted in the nervous literary and social pursuits of self in the modern period.

Mallarmé's extraordinary attentiveness to his period consists in the example which he offers his contemporaries of a disoriented attention. His own historical presence as a literary figure of authority is a lesson in the nonpresentness constitutive of human attention and expression. If, on the one hand, the triptych poems point toward the socializing of a thinker for whom thought is always a response to a particular position in the world, they also help us to understand the apparent remoteness of Mallarmé from the occasions of his occasional writing. The signs of Mallarmé's attention are a moving away from the objects of his attention and the nearly impenetrable terms in which occasions are addressed. In a period obsessed with grasping presence in the present, Mallarmé's inaccessibility is his most serious claim to social relevance. There is no contradiction between the occasional nature of nearly all his writing and his scorn of the immediate.

Mallarmé is perhaps as 'activé par la pression de l'instant' as his contemporaries, but he deprives the instant of its immediacy. For immediacy is an ontological error; the immediacy of sense perverts the nature of thought. The opposite of such immediacy is not 'profound' or non-contingent sense, but rather the moving sense of a thought continuously proposing supplements to the objects abolished by its attention.

Mallarmé asks us to read not statements but the crossing of intervals. He went from a wish to paint the effects of things on him to an attempt to transcribe a fundamentally more impersonal phenomenon of affected perception: not the 'horreur de la forêt' as a particular person experiences it, but the mobility which gets us from forest to, among other things, dread. Difficulty is a function of the ease with which the writer moves. This ease creates a spatial instability which should make us wary of any effort to assimilate Mallarmé to a structuralist esthetic. It is true that he often seems to identify value or authenticity in literature with a kind of structural necessity. The organization of a book defined in ' Le Livre, instrument spirituel,' as the 'hymn' of all relations in the world, would no longer be contaminated by chance (*O.C.*, p. 378). And yet the opposition between chance and necessity seems irrelevant to a view of words 'par le heurt de leur inégalité mobilisés,' that is, to a view of the disruptive effect of verbal juxtapositions on structural stability (*O.C.*, p. 366).[29] The pecularities of Mallarmé's syntax, far from reinforcing structural coherence, set words free from their relational 'necessities.' Mallarmé frequently begins his poems, and even his prose pieces, with de-stabilizing, anti-structural lines in which the principal relations among words are merely relations of shock or collision: A la nue accablante tu..., Quelle soie aux baumes de temps..., Surgi de la croupe et du bond..., Indomptablement a dû..., Victorieusement fui le suicide beau..., and as a start to the essay 'Étalages,' 'Ainsi pas même; ce ne fut: naïf, je commençais à m'y complaire.' To a certain extent, all these pieces go on to coerce their initial words into some sort of structural stability, to return those levitating words to a system of linguistic gravity. But these first lines also define what I take to be a primary intention: that of compelling us not to produce any settled sense at all, of making us experience sense as something which thought is always cancelling, or approaching, or deferring.

Mallarmé rather coquettishly compares the opening and closing of a book to the opening and closing of a fan. A 'site' of meaning is folded back within a closed book as a painted design disappears into the folds of a closed fan. The Book would apparently have consisted of detachable folded pages which the host would have opened in front of his audience. An erotic anticipation of an infinitely precious design or sense hidden within the creases of the fan or the book, as well as the androgynous pleasure of knowing himself to be both the one who penetrates those folds and the one whose reserved sense will be penetrated by others, perhaps even lead Mallarmé to prefer leafing through a book to the reading of books. For when the book is held and agitated as if it were a fan, '...cette autre aile de papier plus vive: infiniment et sommaire en son déploiement, cache le site pour rapporter contre les lèvres une muette fleur peinte comme le mot intact et nul de la songerie par les battements approché' (*O.C.*, p. 374).[30] The intact word which Mallarmé would have us never stop approaching in our reading is null; the excitement of thought is in the movement which both hides and pretends to designate the already inexistent site of sense. *The intervallic sense of the Mallarméan esthetic is the nothingness of consciousness eroticized.* It is the sense of a writer both exceptionally elusive and disarmingly casual and even domestic; a writer who, as in *Quelle soie aux baumes de temps*..., plays with both sex and connotations of military triumph and creates a kind of interstitial sensuality in which both sexual and historical seriousness are gently smothered by a kiss placed, perhaps, somewhere *between* the folds of the silky waving flag of a woman's hair.

Mallarmé's references to the silences of poetry may be thought of as a way of emphasizing the non-adherence of sense to the words which produce sense. The 'reflets réciproques' which light up the words of a poem 'comme une virtuelle traînée de feux sur des pierreries' are those agitations of meaning which blur or silence individual words; they are the 'dazzle' of a signifying process always in excess of, or to the side of, particular signifiers. To produce meaning is to create untranscribable intervals of significance among discreet linguistic units. And yet Mallarmé was also tempted by the possibility of transcribing mobile sense, of transforming the signifying process into fixed visual designs. When, for example, he speaks in 'Crise de vers' of 'des motifs de même jeu' in a poem, motifs which 's'équilibreront, balancés à distance,' he is, I believe, referring not to the fundamental movements by which consciousness is always simultaneously abolishing and resurrecting sense, but rather to a secondary or contingent aspect of the sense-making process in which semantic or phonic repetitions produce diagrammatic sense (*O.C.*, p. 366).[31]

As we can see from the sonnet *Ses purs ongles* and *Un Coup de dés*, Mallarmé was fascinated by an analogy between poetic structures and stellar structures, an analogy which introduced a corrupting structural visibility into his relational esthetic. *Un Coup de dés* is Mallarmé's most impressive effort to stabilize relations, to fix and totalize meaning into a visible hierarchy of semantic privileges. Sequences of lines of various lengths opposite an almost empty page, repetition of the same typography and the same words on the upper left-hand side and the lower right-hand side of two facing pages (I'm thinking of the COMME SI repetition), and pages where different styles of typography alternate with one another: all this produces perceptible designs of sense on every page of Mallarmé's poem. *Un Coup de dés* diagrams intervallic sense.

Mallarmé himself, however, asks us to consider *Un Coup de dés* as a more fluid and dynamic replication of sense-making operations. In his preface to the poem, he claims that the resemblance between *Un Coup de dés* and a musical score is the result of his 'emploi à nu de la pensée avec retraits, prolongements, fuites, ou son dessin même.' 'La mobilité de l'écrit' imitates not any specific content of thought, but the very movement of thought. And, for Mallarmé, the use of the hypothetical in *Un Coup de dés* appears to have been a means of avoiding the distortions imposed on the irregular, 'musical' movement of the mind by a linear narrative progression: 'Tout se passe, par raccourci, en hypothèse; on évite le récit' (*O.C.*, p. 455).[32] Malcom Bowie has made a powerful argument in support of such claims. He speaks of *Un Coup de dés* as 'an exercise in reading which requires of us that we unlearn to read, a mode of discourse where the answers to questions are questions, where dilemmas resolved are dilemmas still, and where the very notion of intelligibility appears to be under threat.' Mallarmé's work gives us 'a world of alternative logics,' and semantic hierarchies which would help us to make 'a neat allegorical diagram' of the poem are notably lacking: 'Steering a ship, casting a die, thinking one's way beyond the limitations of thought – none of these activities has a "natural" priority in the organisation of the poem; none is more elevated or broader in its human scope than the others.'[33] But while there may be alternative meanings in *Un Coup de dés*, meaning itself is definable in fairly clear thematic terms. The congealing of sense into an historico-philosophical thematics in *Un Coup de dés* is prevented neither by the parallel development of themes of physical and intellectual peril, nor by the continuous breaking up of these themes into frequently discontinuous sequences. And, as Robert Greer Cohn has shown in his indispensable study of the poem, the thematizing of sense facilitates a convincing analysis of the work's narrative coherence.[34] Unlike the final version of 'Le Pitre châtié,' *Un Coup de dés* does not subvert a narrativity which at once sustains and is made possible by locatable meanings. Indeed, a major peculiarity of *Un Coup de dés* is that its sense, as Bowie maintains, does remain problematic at the same time that it makes so unmistakenly visible a pattern of thematic parallelisms and a strong line of thematic development.

Un Coup de dés moves between two different types of intervallic sense: stellar-like intervals which can be figured or diagrammed, and the untraceable intervals in which sense is constantly slipping away from any linguistic or visual locatability. This figuration of sense is an immobilizing tactic. It is also a tactic which dissembles the dependence of relational sense on negativity – that is, the dependence of sense on an interval created not by structurable recurrences, but rather by the annihilating movements of consciousness away from all its objects. The typographical signifiers of *Un Coup de dés* can be thought of as the sign of an effort to *correct* the slippage I have just referred to, and to give to the trajectory of meaning a spatial precision and spatial boundaries parallel to the precise alphabetical contours of individual words. Ideally, the meanings of the language of *Un Coup de dés* would be visible on the pages of the poem (intervallic sense would be a phenomenon of typographical spacing), and the signifying process would have taken place – would have a place – outside the untraceable mobility of mental time.

Cantique de Saint Jean

Le soleil que sa halte
Surnaturelle exalte
Aussitôt redescend
Incandescent

Je sens comme aux vertèbres
S'éployer des ténèbres
Toutes dans un frisson
A l'unisson

Et ma tête surgie
Solitaire vigie
Dans les vols triomphaux
De cette faux

Comme rupture franche
Plutôt refoule ou tranche

Igitur, the poet writes

Les anciens désaccords
Avec le corps

Qu'elle de jêunes ivre
S'opiniâtre à suivre
En quelque bond hagard
Son pur regard

Là-haut où la froidure
Eternelle n'endure
Que vous le surpassiez
Tous ô glaciers

Mais selon un baptême
Illuminée au même
Principe qui m'élut
Penche un salut.[35]

Mallarmé may have thought of decapitation as John the Baptist's punishment for daring to look at Hérodiade.[36] He looks at her, and he loses his head. The separation of the head from the rest of the body in the section of *Hérodiade* called 'Cantique de Saint Jean' is a strikingly genial, down-to-earth event. It might, of course, have been the occasion for a movement of transcendence, and it has been argued that in stanza 5 the saint encourages his head to follow his 'pur regard' into heaven.[37] But the poem seems to be saying something far more original: the saint's severed head, *instead of* stubbornly following his look upwards, 'plutôt refoule ou tranche' its former discord with the body. Decapitation provides an opportunity for an unprecedented harmony between mind and body.

But what does it mean to separate the head from the rest of the body without denying the rest of the body? We may remember that in her final words in the *Scène*, Hérodiade accuses her lips of lying and suggests that their 'sanglots suprêmes et meurtris' may be those 'D'une enfance sentant parmi les rêveries/ Se séparer enfin ses froides pierreries.'[38] The adolescent's awakening to sexuality is a kind of articulation of consciousness, a movement of separation, or the creation of spaces between the 'cold precious stones' of her reveries. It is as if John, in looking at Hérodiade with desire, had moved her into a state of self-division, had penetrated and opened the folds of her mind with something of the violence which Mallarmé imagined in a paper-knife's 'bloody' opening of a book's closed pages (*O.C.*, p. 381). The saint's punishment is nothing more than a version of his crime. It inaccurately replicates the crime of his desire in a mode which illuminates the nature of desire. Desire is a *cosa mentale*, a thing of the head; it is a separation from the body which, however, articulates the continuities between mind and body.

The 'Cantique de Saint Jean' is a way of thinking the saint's desires, and it thinks those desires as an almost indescribable movement of the head. The saint's head has 'surged up' in the scythe's 'triumphant flights': as we can also see in the prose poem 'Pauvre enfant pâle,' Mallarmé seems to imagine decapitation as the release of a spring which catapults the head upwards. But Saint John's head describes an arc: having sprung up away from his body, it then curves downward. And this strangely leaning fall of the now divinely illuminated head is a 'salut': at once a salvation and a greeting. The fall by which the saint enters heaven is also his severed head's comically charming gesture of salutation to the world. The living saint's passionate looking at Hérodiade has been transformed into an impersonal, generalized and posthumous sociability. Saint John's decapitation recapitulates his passion *as* sociability. It reflects (on) desire's power of separation as a modulation of desire's intensity, and it therefore suggests that desire is already a supplemental movement away from the presumed objects of desire, a separating movement which simultaneously tames and abstracts. In short, the 'Cantique de Saint Jean' is a monologic fable of sublimation. But its great originality is to propose that desire, far from being disguised and disciplined by sublimation, is by nature an act of sublimation. Desire produces sublimation; to de-sublimate desire is to erase it.

To speak of art as a primary sublimating activity should therefore be understood not as a way of defining the esthetic in terms of a 'raising up,' a making sublime, of sensual impulses, but rather as a means of drawing attention to what I have called the differential moves of eroticized thought in art. 'L'Après-midi d'un faune' is especially instructive about the immediate esthetic productivity of desire. The faun begins by worrying that he may have loved only a 'dream,' but soon it becomes clear that whether or not the nymphs were really there makes no difference for either the making of music or the renewal of desire. The faun's wish to describe the nymphs is profitably, and nonchalantly, confused with his efforts to remember them. He doesn't move from sexual desire to art; both desire and art are nothing, but the hopelessly problematic relation between the world and both esthetic and erotically stimulated inventions have the effect not of discouraging the faun, but of increasing his appetites in a world he cannot know.

As in *Hérodiade*, the activity of desire is presented as a kind of criminal separation in 'L'Après-midi d'un faune.' The faun is guilty of having '*divisé la touffe échevelée / De baisers que les dieux gardaient si bien mêlée.*'[39] The nymphs' embrace can perhaps be thought of as an erotic analogue to the opaque, undifferentiated consciousness to which Igitur aspires. The phallic 'line' with which the faun separates the two nymphs initiates a process of fertile self-division, of moving away from the chimerical unity of specular being. The faun's 'crime' is the precondition for living thought. But, as in the sonnets of the triptych, the differentiations which nourish sensuality and art remain resolutely solipsistic in 'L'Après-midi d'un faune.' The narcissistic eroticism of the nymphs is replaced with the faun's erotic relation – to himself. The faun's narcissism, and Mallarméan solipsism in general, are the logical, if unexpected, correlatives of Mallarmé's unshakeable belief in the reality of the external world. To recall the striking formulas of 'La Musique et les lettres': 'n'est que ce qui est', and 'La Nature a lieu, ou n'y ajoutera pas.' Only the material world *is*, but consciousness establishes relations only within its own continuously negativized fictions. The very sign of Mallarmé's belief in the world – as well as of the faun's exuberant appetites – is the proliferation of solipsistic fictions. Even if the nymphs had been real, the faun would have had to invent them. The fiction of a definitive relation to the world is the symptom of an immobilized, specular narcissism. Mallarmé's faun ingratiatingly authorizes us to separate those two words and to speak of a nonspecular narcissism, as well as of a solipsism which, far from perpetuating sameness, ceaselessly produces difference.[40]

Even more astonishingly, the faun invites us, by the rich 'idolatrous portrayals' which supplement and dismiss real nymphs, to conceive of an irony no longer constrained by ironic reservations. At the beginning of this study, I quoted from a letter to Henri Cazalis in which Mallarmé complains of having come upon the 'abyss' of 'Nothingness' during his work on *Hérodiade*. While composing the 'glorious lies' of poetry, he experiences his own being as merely a vain form of matter. More significant than the philosophical rhetoric of that letter is the self-divisive experience which it records. Not only is Mallarmé's work separated from his being; the poet moves away from this separation into a consciousness of the split between poetry and being as a 'sublime spectacle.' Writing verse, I suggested, multiplies distances for Mallarmé; it generates an ironic consciousness of poetry. In 'L'Après-midi d'un faune,' a productive receding of consciousness is exactly equivalent to the sublimating movements by which the faun makes music from his desire:

> Mais, bast! arcane tel élut pour confident
> Le jonc vaste et jumeau dont sous l'azur on joue:
> Qui, détournant à soi le trouble de la joue,
> Rêve, dans un solo long, que nous amusions
> La beauté d'alentour par des confusions
> Fausses entre elle-même et notre chant crédule;
> Et de faire aussi haut que l'amour se module
> Evanouir du songe ordinaire de dos
> Ou de flanc pur suivis avec mes regards clos,
> Une sonore, vaine et monotone ligne.[41]

The faun's reed turns away from, replicates, supplements, and modulates his sensuality. And yet the 'long solo' of his musical dream is not the fictive 'line' of music which could be read as the esthetic distillation of his sensual fantasies of a nymph's back or 'flanc pur.' His solo *dreams of* making that distillation take place. That is, the faun's art is not the metamorphic replication of bodily lines as lines of music, but rather the suspension and deferral of that esthetic abstraction in an anticipatory consciousness of it. The possibility of treating art as symbolic representations of sensual impulses is therefore ruined by the agitations of the 'symbolizing' consciousness itself. More precisely, the sublimating consciousness described by the faun operates on what might be called a principle of accelerating supplementarity. And the consequence of this process of acceleration is that symbolic equivalences are never more than a step in the supplemental movements of thought. The faun profoundly suggests that the reflection of his erotic fantasies in his music is a mobilizing project of his art rather than its actual sense. That reflection may be the purpose of his art, but his performance of art depends on the suspension of its purpose, on a slippage of sense from the evoked, unperformed, and oppressively significant 'line' to the space between it and the 'dream' which has in fact already retreated from any such settled sense in dismissively anticipating it.

The faun moves from wondering if he desired a mere dream to dreaming, in the long solo of his music, that nature was charmed by his confusion between his dream and her. During the 'prélude lent où naissent les pipeaux' he had seen 'ce vol de cygnes, non! de naïades.'[42] But to remember them is to wonder if he really saw them. But to doubt their reality is to wish to paint them, and to paint them is to return to his desires, and to confuse, once again, what he desires with what may really be there. In this pseudo-circle which appears to return the faun to his musical point of departure, but which really moves him from an art of entrapped realism to an art of happily mobile ironies, the faun 'revises' his having been seduced by his own art by including, within that art, his sense of nature having been beguiled by his credulous song's confusions. In one sense, that seduction of the surrounding natural beauty is the faun's ironic snapping away from his own naïveté. It is the reservation hidden within the subsequent account of the faun's sexual assault on the nymphs, the potentially annihilating awareness of that assault as mere illusion. And yet nothing is annihilated. The faun's 'remembered' erotic violence is somewhat modified by our own uncertainty about where or who the faun is. He is the perpetrator of violence, but he is also nature's response to a fiction of violence. The irony of 'L'Après-midi d'un faune' is additive rather than corrosive. It both removes the faun from the nymphs and returns him to them, and, far from undermining his desire, it makes the objects of desire productively unlocatable.

'L'Aprés-midi d'un faune' performs sublimation as a mode of Mallarmé's irony. Mallarmé encourages us to view sublimation not as a mechanism by which desire is denied but rather as a self-reflexive activity by which desire multiplies and diversifies its representations. There is, to be sure, a certain purification of the desiring impulse, but purification should be understood here as an abstracting rather than a desexualizing process. The faun's sexual brutality is modulated by the doubt inherent in the account of his brutality; his attack is both negativized and enjoyed once again by an analytic and critical recitation of the attack. In reading that the nymphs try to escape from the faun's arms 'Pour fuir ma lèvre en feu buvant, comme un éclair/Tressaille! la frayeur secrète de la chair,'[43] we may – inappropriately yet also aptly – remember the etymological sense of sublimation: a transformation by fire of a solid into a gas. The quivering flame of the faun's lips explodes the still unity of the nymphs' bodies. But the faun himself is divided and devoured by the ironic passion of Mallarmé's poem. In his willful re-creation of scenes which may never have taken place, the faun narcissistically indulges a self already burned away. Desire purifies the faun of his identity. It 'drinks' the secret fright of a person, just as the poet's sublimating speech divides the writer from himself, dissipates the oppressive themes of his being in the exuberant irony of his work. With a sophistication worthy of his creator, Mallarmé's faun ironically offers us the coolness of art in his surely mistaken memories of the terror inspired by a tongue on fire.

NOTES

Foreword

1 *L'Univers imaginaire de Mallarmé* (Paris: Editions du Seuil, 1961), p. 13.

2 That this demonstration is also made – ambivalently, unwillingly – by Freud himself will be the argument of another book. Much of the work on the present book was made possible by a Fellowship from the National Endowment for the Humanities.

I. The man dies

1 *Stéphane Mallarmé, Correspondance 1862–1871*, ed. Henri Mondor (Paris: Gallimard, 1959), pp. 207–8. Cited in the text as *C*.

I will finally have realized my dream: to write a poem worthy of Poe and just as good as his. ... Unfortunately, in delving so far into verse, I have come upon two abysses, which are driving me to despair.

Yes, *I know* that we are only empty forms of matter, empty and yet sublime for we have invented God and our soul. So sublime, my friend, that I want to offer myself this spectacle of matter conscious of its own being and yet plunging frantically into the Dream which it knows does not exist, singing of the Soul and all such divine impressions stored up in us since the earliest times, and proclaiming, in the face of the Nothing which is truth, those glorious lies!

All translations from Mallarmé are my own. Since the syntax of Mallarmé's prose is frequently at least as idiosyncratic as that of his verse, it has seemed best to give all my quotations from his work in French, in spite of the obviously awkward movement in my text between French and English which this choice entails. I have aimed at nothing more in my translations than to provide English-speaking readers with the 'literal' sense of the French text most consistent with my interpretive reading of it. I am fully aware how problematic Mallarmé renders the notion of literal translation; in fact, having done these translations and consulted the brave efforts of several others, I am, a bit desperately and a bit lightheadedly, quite ready to argue that

Mallarmé proposes not merely the impossibility but even the *inconceivability* of translation. I am grateful to Eléonore Zimmerman for her generous help in this unimaginable task.

2 ...the mere physical act of writing sets off an attack of hysteria...I am still not entirely over my crisis, since giving dictation to my faithful secretary, and the impression of a pen moving as a result of *my* will (even though its movements depend on someone else's hand) bring back my palpitations.

four prose poems, on the spiritual conception of Nothingness...'the totality of literary works which make up the poetic existence of a Dreamer' and which is called, finally, his *œuvre*.

3 Mallarmé, *Œuvres complètes*, ed. Henri Mondor and G. Jean-Aubry (Paris: Gallimard, Bibliothèque de la Pléiade, 1945), pp. 365–6. A new, truly complete edition of Mallarmé's work is badly needed; the Pléiade volume – curiously mistitled, poorly organized, and unhelpfully annotated – will be cited in my text as *O.C.*

in fear and trembling, for I am inventing a language which must spring from a completely new poetics that might be briefly defined in the following way: *Describe not the object itself, but the effect which it produces.*

therefore, a line of verse must not be made up of words, but rather of intentions; all the words must retreat and be replaced by sensations.

an intimate and peculiar way of painting and setting down very rapid impressions

the dread of the forest or the silent thunder scattered through the foliage; not the intrinsic and dense wood of the trees.

4 every soul is a rhythmic knot.

some secret pursuit of music, within the margins of Discourse.

Also, in 'La Musique et les lettres,' we read: 'Style, versification, s'il y a cadence et c'est pourquoi toute prose d'écrivain fastueux, soustraite à ce laisser-aller en usage, ornementale, vaut en tant qu'un vers rompu, jouant avec ses timbres et encore les rimes dissimulées: selon un thyrse plus complexe' (*O.C.*, p. 644).

As long as there is cadence, there will be style, and versification; and that is why the prose of any sumptuous writer – an ornamental prose with none of the carelessness now in vogue – can be thought of as broken verse, playing with its tonal qualities and its hidden rhymes: like a more complex thyrsus.

5 Almost a year later, Mallarmé will make the same announcement ('...je suis parfaitement mort...') in writing to Cazalis (*C.*, p. 240).

6 ...Everything is so well ordered in me that each of my sensations is at once transfigured and finds its place, on its own, in a particular book and a particular poem. When a poem is ripe, it will fall away from me.

You see that I am imitating natural law...the center of my being, where I am sitting like a sacred spider, on the main threads already spun out from my mind, threads which will help me to weave at the *intersecting points* marvelous lacework, which I can imagine, and which already exist in the heart of Beauty.

7 ...I am now impersonal and no longer the Stéphane you once knew, but one of the ways the spiritual Universe has of seeing itself and developing, through what used to be me. Given the fragility of my ghostly presence on earth, I can only develop in ways absolutely necessary for the Universe to recapture, in that self, its identity.

8 truly fragmented, and to think that's necessary for me to have a very – unified view of the Universe! Otherwise, the only unity one feels is that of one's own life.

...I tried to stop thinking with my head and, with a desperate effort, I stiffened all the nerves in my chest in order to produce a vibration, still holding onto the thought I was then working on, which becomes the subject of that vibration, or an impression – and in that state I sketched an entire poem which I had been dreaming of for a long time.

9 By the first two sections, I mean the 'Ouverture ancienne' and the 'Scène.' Only the 'Scène' was published in Mallarmé's lifetime; his son-in-law, Dr Edward Bonniot, published the 'Ouverture ancienne' in 1926. It appears, however, that both these sections were written between 1864 and 1866. In *Les Noces d'Hérodiade* (Paris: Gallimard, 1959), Gardner Davies both discusses the forms which Mallarmé's definitive version of the poem might have taken, and presents sections not available in the Pléiade edition of Mallarmé's work.

10 reflects in its slumbering calm / Hérodiade with the clear diamantine look.

11 Reported by Jean-Pierre Richard in *L'Univers imaginaire de Mallarmé* (Paris: Aux Editions du Seuil, 1961), p. 518.

12 These remarks on consciousness and negativity obviously raise the issue of Hegel's influence on Mallarmé. I am, however, less interested in discussing this question – abundantly treated elsewhere – than in following the rather simple if radical logic of an experience of consciousness which could also be, as it were, academically located in a history of philosophy. My development here has parallels to Maurice Blanchot's contention that for Mallarmé 'authentic language' annihilates the absent object; the word's function is 'not only representative, but destructive' (*La Part du feu* [Paris: Gallimard, 1949], p. 37).

13 I have just spent a terrifying year: my Thought thought itself and reached a pure conception.

14 The nurse, speaking of Hérodiade's room, describes:

sa tapisserie, au lustre nacré, plis
Inutiles avec les yeux ensevelis
De sibylles offrant leur ongle vieil aux Mages.

Une d'elles, avec un passé de ramages
Sur ma robe blanchie en l'ivoire fermé
Au ciel d'oiseaux parmi l'argent noir parsemé,
Semble, de vols [partis] costumée et fantôme,
Un arôme qui porte, ô roses! un arôme,
Loin du lit vide qu'un cierge soufflé cachait,
Un arôme d'[os] froids rôdant sur le sachet,
Une touffe de fleurs parjures à la lune
(A la cire expirée encor s'effeuille l'une),
De qui le long regret et les tiges de qui
Trempent en un seul verre à l'éclat alangui.

its tapestry, with pearly lustre, useless / Folds with the buried eyes / Of sibyls offering their old fingernails to the Magi. / One of them, with floral embroidery / On my bleached dress locked in the ivory chest / With a bird-filled sky amid the black silver, / Seems, in a costume of departed flights and phantom-like, / An aroma which carries, oh roses! an aroma, / Far from the empty bed hidden by a blown-out candle, / An aroma of cold bones prowling on the sachet, / A bunch of flowers unfaithful to the moon / (By the extinguished candle one of them is still shedding its petals), / Whose long regret and whose stems / Stand in a single glass with languid glitter.

15 The Pléiade edition has 'ors' instead of 'os' (and 'Semble, de vols partir...' instead of 'Semble, de vols partis...' in the passage translated in note 14). But I am adopting Davies' reading of the 'Ouverture.'

16 *La Poésie de Stéphane Mallarmé* (Paris: Gallimard, 1926), p. 388. In this edition, Thibaudet mentions the 'Ouverture ancienne,' published by Bonniot in 1926, but Thibaudet's work was written in 1911, and his comments undoubtedly refer to the 'Scène.'

17 Abolished, and its frightful wing in the tears / Of the pool, abolished, that mirrors the alarms, / Thrashing the crimson space of naked gold, / A Dawn has, heraldic plumage, chosen / Our cinerary and sacrificial tower, / Heavy tomb which a beautiful bird has fled, solitary / Caprice of dawn with vain black plumage...

18   L'eau morne se résigne,
Que ne visite plus la plume ni le cygne
Inoubliable

The gloomy water resigns itself, / No longer touched by a feather or by the unforgettable / Swan

19 desolated / By the pure diamond of a star, but / Long ago, and which never sparkled

Unknown golds, keeping their ancient light / Under the somber sleep of a primeval earth

20 Albert Sonnenfeld has subtly studied, in an early version of *Victorieuse-ment fui le suicide beau* and in 'L'Après-midi d'un faune,' a 'pattern of disappearing vision' which he traces to the 'original erotic inspiration'

of Mallarmé's adolescent *priapisme* (see 'Eros and Poetry: Mallarmé's Disappearing Visions,' in *Order and Adventure in French Post-Romantic Poetry* [New York: Oxford University Press, 1976], p. 94).

21 *L'Univers imaginaire de Mallarmé*, p. 599. See Jacques Derrida's critique of the dialectical intention inherent in Richard's thematic criticism, in the essay 'La Double Séance' in *La Dissémination* (Paris: Editions du Seuil, 1972), p. 276ff.

22 For her eyes, – to swim in those lakes, on whose embankments / Are planted beautiful eyelashes which a blue morning penetrates, / I have, Muse, – I, your clown, – climbed through the window / And fled our tents where your oil lamps are smoking.

And drunk from grasses, I dove like a traitor / Into those forbidden lakes, and, when you called me, / I bathed my naked limbs in the water filled with white pebbles, / Forgetting my clown's costume on the trunk of a beech tree.

The morning sun was drying my new body / And, far from your tyranny, I felt / The snow from the glaciers cooling in my purified flesh,

Unaware, alas, when the soot from my hair and the paint from my body were carried away by the water, / Muse, that all my genius was in that dirt! (Version of 1864)

Eyes, lakes [nets] with, simply, my drunken wish to be reborn / Different from the clownish actor who through his gestures called forth / As feather the ignoble soot of the oil lamps, / I have ripped through the canvas wall a window.

A limpid traitorous swimmer with my arms and legs, / With numerous leaps, repudiating the bad / Hamlet! it is as if I were creating in the water / A thousand tombs in which – a virgin – to disappear.

Laughing cymbal-gold with fists irritated, / All at once the sun strikes the nudity / Which, pure, emanated from my pearly cool freshness,

Rancid night of the skin when you passed over me, / Not knowing ungrateful one! that my entire consecration lay in / That paint now drowned in the treacherous water of the glaciers. (Version of 1887)

23 *The Art of the Novel*, ed. Richard P. Blackmur (New York and London: Charles Scribner's Sons, 1934), p. 389.

II. Poetry is buried

1 too obsolete and seething with preparations for [the poet] to have anything else to do but work in secret with an eye to later on or never.

his calling card, some stances or a sonnet, in order not to be stoned by them, if they suspected him of knowing that they don't exist.
personal work... will be anonymous, for in it the Text will speak by itself and without an author's voice.

2 See Le '*Livre*' *de Mallarmé* (Paris: Gallimard, 1957). A. R. Chisholm has argued, against Scherer, that the Work is not something distinct from the poems actually finished by Mallarmé. The written work is part of, contributes to, an ideal Book. The latter would not be a real volume, but 'something that goes on' (Mallarmé's 'Grand *Œuvre*' [Manchester University Press, 1962], p. 6). I sympathize with these remarks, although, as I will presently suggest, they should make the very notion of an 'ideal Book' (to which however, the fragments published by Scherer do seem to point...) superfluous.

3 *Correspondance II 1871–1885*, ed. Henri Mondor and Lloyd James Austin (Paris: Gallimard, 1965), p. 37.

...I want to sing, in rhymed couplets, of one of Gautier's glorious virtues: the mysterious gift of seeing with his eyes (take out mysterious). I will sing of the *seer*, who, put in this world, looked at it, which is not done.

4 The Master, by his deep eye, has, as he went, / Soothed Eden's uneasy wonder / Whose final shiver, in his voice alone, awakens / For the Rose and the Lily the mystery of a name. / Is there nothing of this destiny which remains? / Oh all of you, forget a somber creed. / Splendid eternal genius has no shadow. / Concerned about your desire, I want to see / Him who vanished, yesterday, in the ideal / Duty created for us by the gardens of this star, / Survived for the honor of the calm disaster / By a solemn agitation through the air / Of words, drunken purple and large clear calyx, / Which, rain and diamond, the diaphanous look / Remaining there on those flowers not one of which fades, / Isolates amid the hour and the light of the day!

5 The poet's Platonism is perhaps also gently mocked by the smile of a 'sensible and tender sister,' as well as by the sepulchre's laugh, in the last stanza of 'Prose,' at the notion of a non-ephemeral, immortal beauty. Malcolm Bowie acutely discusses the Platonism of the poem in *Mallarmé and the Art of Being Difficult* (Cambridge: Cambridge University Press, 1978), pp. 25–31 and 78–83. 'The mood of "Prose pour des Esseintes",' Bowie writes, 'is by turns exalted and quizzical, and the great metaphysical question which it reformulates is kept alive throughout by a delicate pattern of assertions and reiterated doubts' (p. 26).

6 Yes, on an island where the air is heavy / With sight and not with visions / Every flower spread itself out more boldly / Without our speaking of it.

So that, immense, each one / In its turn adorned itself / With clear outlines, a hiatus, / Which separated it from the gardens.

My translation of *ordinairement* as 'in its turn' follows Émilie Noulet's suggestion that only the Latin sense of the adverb allows us to understand the preterite *para*. 'Ordinarily' or 'commonly' would seem to have required the imperfect *parait*. (*Vingt Poèmes de Stéphane Mallarmé* [Genève: Droz, 1967], p. 122).

7   Oh let the Spirit of litigation know, / At this hour of our silence, / That with multiple lilies the stem / Was growing too much for our reasons.

And not as the shore weeps, / When its monotonous game lies / In wishing for amplitude to arrive [does not / Wish amplitude to arrive] / Amid my youthful wonderment

At hearing all the sky and the map / Which my steps ceaselessly attest, / By the very waves which part, / That this land did not exist.

This is one of the most difficult passages in Mallarmé's poetry. Exegetical differences tend to converge on the connotations of 'ampleur' (see Camille Soula, *Gloses sur Mallarmé* [Paris: Editions Diderot, 1946], p. 44; Noulet, *Vingt Poèmes de Stéphane Mallarmé*, pp. 110–11; Cohn, *Toward the Poems of Mallarmé*, pp. 252–3; Richard, *L'Univers imaginaire de Mallarmé*, pp. 332–3; L. J. Austin, 'Mallarmé, Huysmans et la "Prose pour des Esseintes",' in *Revue d'histoire littéraire de la France*, vol. 54, no. 2 (avril–juin 1954), pp. 173–5.

8   Greeting of madness and pale libation, / Do not think that I offer my empty cup, where a golden monster suffers, to the magic hope of the corridor!

9   And we cannot but know that this beautiful monument, chosen for the very simple celebration at which we are singing the poet's absence, holds all of him.

Another example – and I of course am giving only a few of them – of a debatable translation. Many readers will insist that 'ce beau monument' refers to Gautier's tomb. I see no objection to this, but neither do I see any reason to reject Noulet's suggestion – adopted here – that the expression refers to the volume of poems in Gautier's honor (see *Vingt Poèmes de Stéphane Mallarmé*, p. 13). Davies, however, insists that the tomb must be the tomb containing Gautier's body (see *Les "Tombeaux" de Mallarmé*, [Paris: Librairie José Corti], pp. 25–6).

10 the solid sepulchre where everything harmful lies, / Both the miserly silence and the massive night.

11 *Mallarmé l'Obscur* (Paris: Editions Denoël, 1941), pp. 169–70.

12 See *Magies de Verlaine* (Paris: Librairie José Corti, 1967).

13 Verse has been tampered with.
    ...the act of writing was scrutinized it its very orgin...much greater than any renewal of rites and rhymes.

14 the sharpening, toward their engraved expression, of ideas in all areas.

everything which proceeds from the mind returns to the mind.

Nature is, we will not add anything to it...

Prisoners of an absolute formula, we know that, to be sure, only that which is, is.

and, if you like, alone, to the exclusion of everything else.

15 See note 4 in Chapter 1.

16 in the literary history of any nation, in conjunction with the general and age-old great organ effects of orthodox verse pouring forth from a latent keyboard, anyone, with his individual technique and ear, can build his own instrument, as soon as he blows into it, touches it lightly or strikes it knowledgeably; play it separately and dedicate it also to Language. It should be pointed out that the Pléiade edition, as Norman Paxton points out, gives 'a rather garbled account' of how 'Crise de vers' was put together. See Paxton's clarifying summary of the architecture of this piece in *The Development of Mallarmé's Prose Style* (Geneva: Librairie Droz, 1968), pp. 88–9.

17 extinction, or rather a wear-and-tear to the point of showing the thread... orgiastic periodic excesses.

... the retempering process, generally hidden, is taking place publicly, by the return to delightful approximations.

18 pure work [which] implies the disappearance of the poet's voice, and the initiative is taken by the words themselves.

stammered out the magic concept of the Work.

the law of the world... The differences between individual works offering so many versions put forth in a vast collaboration to create the true text, between those periods called civilized or – highly literate.

19 flies, beyond the individual volume, to several other poets who are placing, on spiritual space, the amplified stamp of genius, as anonymous and perfect as a work of art.

20 Languages are imperfect because multiple, the supreme one is missing

to write without accessories, even without whispering, the immortal word being still silent.

regrets that words fail to express objects with touches that would be faithful to the coloring or aspect of objects.

As Gérard Genette has written: 'Language, even poetic language – especially poetic language, – has better things to do than imitate the world....' The 'necessity' which Mallarmé seeks to oppose to chance is something different from a mimetic relation of the word to the world (*Mimologiques* [Paris: Editions du Seuil, 1976], p. 277).

21 something other than known calyxes.

musically arises, the idea itself – exquisite and sweet – the absent one from all bouquets.

the constraint of a close and concrete reminder... a pure idea.

22 For Mallarmé, Blanchot writes, the poet 'does not substitute the ideal presence of an object for its real absence' (*La Part du feu*, p. 38).

23 to take or to put a coin silently in someone else's hand.

The notes for the Book, it is true, indicate an extraordinarily ambitious project of communication. But it would certainly not be the personal thoughts or feelings of the poet which would be communicated. Even when Mallarmé dreams of communication, he does not have in mind the Proustian transparency of individual souls.

24 *Remembrance of Things Past*, tr. C. K. Scott-Moncrieff, 2 vols (New York: Random House, 1924), II, pp. 559, 558, 490 and 559. Pages given in the order of the quotations in this paragraph.

25 Far from having the function of an easily exchanged and clearly representative currency, as it does first of all with the masses, speech, above all dream and song, recovers thanks to the Poet, out of a necessity inherent in an act devoted to fictions, its virtuality.

26 natural materials and, as something brutal, the ordering of these materials by precise thought; and this is done in order to retain only the suggestiveness of things.

out of a handful of dust or any reality, and without confining it to a book (even considered as a text), that volatile scattering which is spirit, and which cares for nothing except the musicality of everything.

on the fine paper of the volume anything but for example the dread of the forest, or the silent thunder scattered through the foliage; not the intrinsic and dense wood of the trees.

27 *Mallarmé et la musique* (Paris: Librairie Nizet, 1959), p. 35.

28 the means of transposing the symphony to the Book, or quite simply, of getting back our rightful due: for it is not from the elementary sounds made by brasses, strings or woodwinds, but, undeniably, from the language of intellect at its highest point of expression that, with fulness and clarity, understood as the totality of relations existing in everything, Music should proceed.

29 All that we can do, and all that we will ever be able to do, is to seize relationships, occasional, however scarce or numerous.

30 in harmony with some inner state which one may wish to extend at will, to simplify the world.

silent melodic figuring of those motifs which, with the very fibers of our being, compose a logical structure.

III. Igitur, the poet writes

1 At moments of want or to get the money for ruinously expensive boats, I have had to take on some respectable jobs (Dieux Antiques, Mots Anglais), which it would be best not to mention; but aside from that the concessions I've made to necessity as well as to pleasure have not been numerous.

2 See Genette's discussion of *Les Mots anglais* in *Mimologiques*, and Judy

Kravis' interesting discussion of *La Dernière mode* in *The Prose of Mallarmé: The Evolution of a Literary Language* (Cambridge: Cambridge University Press, 1976).

3 however successful one of their [a word is missing] may sometimes be, they barely make up an album, but not a book.

propelled by the pressure of the moment...the cloud, [which is] precious, floating over the secret abyss of every thought...the common may be defined as that on which one confers the attribute of immediacy, and nothing more.

4 In *L'Œuvre poétique de Stéphane Mallarmé*, pp. 37–45.

5 can still set me to dreaming for a long while when I dust them off

6 What a performance! It contains the world. If a book which we are holding sets forth some august idea, that book takes the place of all theaters, not by making us forget them, but, on the contrary, by imperiously recalling them.

he who confines himself to the humble and sacred expedients of language

an opera without any accompaniment or singing, one that is spoken; now the book will try to suffice, in order to half-open the inner stage and whisper its echoes. A versified whole invites us to an ideal performance....

an intelligence, having taken refuge within several pages of a book, [which] defies a civilization neglecting to build – so that they may take place – the prodigious Theater and the Stage which that intelligence dreams of.

7 in a single stroke – which is exactly what we should see in order not to be inconvenienced by their presence.

8 Everything is steeped and reinvigorated in the primitive stream: but not back to the source. This will not be the way in which the strictly imaginative and abstract, and therefore poetic, French mind shines forth. It shrinks away from Legend, and thereby is at one with pure art, which is invention. Take note of the French failing to preserve any over-sized and unpolished anecdote from bygone days; it is as if they sensed how anachronistic any such anecdote would be in a theatrical representation, in the consecrating Rite of an act of Civilization.

The Exhibition and Transmission of Powers, etc. would I see Brunhilde in such ceremonies; and you, Siegfried, what role could you possibly play in them!

disengaged from personality, for that myth constitutes our multiplicity ...a spiritual fact, the blossoming of symbols or their preparation...our dreams of sites or of paradise...reciprocal proofs...his authentic earthly home.

9 Some supreme flash of lightning, which gives birth to the figure which is No One

the fictive center of vision shot forth by the gaze of a crowd.

10 *Le 'Livre' de Mallarmé*, pp. 107–A, 189–A, and 96. And yet none of this changes Scherer's view of the noncontingent nature of the Book's content. 'In order to write the Book, it will be necessary to be completely delivered from circumstance.' And: 'Ordinary books are circumstantial; the Book will not be attached to any particular object and will deal with the totality of existing things' (pp. 17 and 22).

11 but it burst forth, forced out by the brutal blow to the stomach caused by the impatience of people to whom, at whatever cost and suddenly, something must be proclaimed, even if it is only a reverie...

Barbara Johnson subtly points out that '...it is not the hair or any of its symbolic substitutes which is being discussed in the concluding dialogue of ["La Déclaration foraine"], but rather the conditions of possibility of the emission and reception of the sonnet itself' ('Poetry and Performative Language,' *Yale French Studies* 54, p. 142). In the same issue of *Yale French Studies* – an issue devoted entirely to Mallarmé – Albert Sonnenfeld uses 'La Déclaration foraine' in an interesting argument – quite different from mine – for performance as 'profanation,' and for 'an increasingly ironic tonality [in the poem], the purpose of which seems to be to demean the progressively emerging public theatrical function' (see pp. 168–72).

Mallarmé's prose poems have been subjected to much less exegetical attention than his verse, so it seems appropriate to mention Ursula Franklin's fine reading of 'La Déclaration foraine' in *An Anatomy of Poesis: The Prose Poems of Stéphane Mallarmé* (Chapel Hill: North Carolina Studies in the Romance Languages and Literatures, No. 16, 1976).

12 'The Difficulties of Modernism and the Modernism of Difficulty,' *Humanities in Society*, Vol. 1, No. 2 (Spring 1978), p. 272.

13 In fact, with regard to those supreme or intact aristocracies which we were maintaining, literature and the arts, the pretense of a need, almost a cult, has started: people turn away, esthetically, from the intermediate games offered to the majority of the public, and toward the exception and any lesser sign, with everyone anxious to proclaim himself capable of understanding anything rare.

a residue of the old-fashioned combats of generous and baroque spirits or in conformity with society, of which literature is the unmediated refinement – ...in order to maintain their integrity.

14 'The Difficulties of Modernism and the Modernism of Difficulty,' pp. 227, 279 and 281.

15 *Ibid*, p. 281.

16 Mallarmé uses the expression in describing those constantly shifting

positions of groups which constitute the 'first subject,' and the meaning, of dance (*O.C.*, p. 304).

17 (Harmondsworth, Middlesex and Baltimore, Md.: Penguin Books, 1966), p. 517.

18 a movement...persists, recognizable as more pressing by a double stroke, which no longer reaches, or has not yet reached, its idea...the perfect symmetry of the foreseen deductions gave the lie to

This time, no longer any doubt; certainty is reflected in absolutely clear facts. If the vision of a place continued to appear, it was in vain, merely the reminiscence of a lie of which this vision was the consequence, a vision such as the expected interval was supposed to be, having, in fact, as lateral walls the double placing of the panels opposite each other, and as facing walls, both in front and behind, the doubt-free opening both reverberated by the prolongation of the noise of the panels, where the plumage is fleeing, and doubled by the explored ambiguity. Thus the perfect symmetry of the foreseen deductions gave the lie to the reality of the vision of a place; there was no mistaking it, it was self-consciousness (for which even the absurd could serve as a place) – its successful realization.

19 constrained by perfect self-certainty...and to return into itself, into its opacity.

on the opposite walls, which reflected each other, two gaping openings made by a massive shadow which must of necessity have been the opposite of these shadows, not their appearance but their disappearance, the negative shadow of themselves.

20 I don't like this sound: this perfection of my certainty bothers me: everything is too clear, which reveals the desire of an escape; everything is too bright, I would like to return within my uncreated and anterior shadow, and shed, through an act of thought, the disguise imposed on me by my having to live in the heart of this race (which I hear beating here) the only remaining ambiguity.

21 a persona whose thought is not aware of him...my final form, separated from its persona by a spider-like ruff and a form which does not know itself. Thus, now that the duality of my persona is forever separated, and that I no longer even hear through him the sound of his progress, I am going to forget myself through him, and dissolve within myself.

22 *L'Espace littéraire* (Paris: Gallimard, 1955), pp. 145 and 136.

I

23 Does all Pride turn to smoke in the evening, [Does all pride of the evening turn to smoke], / A torch snuffed out by a shake / Without the immortal puff of smoke / Being able to delay the desertion!

The old chamber of the heir / Of many a rich but fallen trophy / Would not even be heated / Were he to come through the hall.

Necessary agonies of the past / Gripping as if with claws / Disavowal's sepulchre,

Under the heavy marble it isolates / No other fire is lit / Than the flashing console.

II

Risen from the rump and the bound / Of an ephemeral glassware / Without adorning with a flower the bitter vigil / The unknown [ignored] neck stops short.

I think that two mouths have never / Drunk, neither her lover nor my mother, / From the same Chimera, / I, sylph of this cold ceiling!

The pure, unsoiled vase which has known no drink / Other than the inexhaustible widowhood / Agonizes, but does not consent,

Naïve funereal kiss! / To breathe out anything announcing / A rose in the darkness.

III

A lace [curtain] is abolished / In the doubt of the supreme Game / Half-opening like a blasphemy / Only eternal absence of a bed.

This unrelieved white conflict / Of a garland with its like / Having fled onto the pale pane / Is floating more than burying.

But, in whoever gilds himself with dream / Sadly sleeps a mandolin / With a hollow musical nothingness

[A mandolin] such that by some window / Along no belly but its own, / Filial one might have been born.

24   *Vingt poèmes de Stéphane Mallarmé*, p. 155.
25   Each of several interpretations of this line has its exegetical partisans in Mallarmé scholarship. Émilie Noulet (*L'Œuvre poétique de Stéphane Mallarmé*, p. 437) and Gardner Davies (*Mallarmé et le drame solaire* [Paris: Librairie José Corti, 1959], p. 194) see in 'du soir' a genitive construction ('tout Orgueil du soir fume...'). Cohn (*Toward the Poems of Mallarmé*, p. 197) translates 'du soir' as an adverbial phrase ('Does all Pride [turn to] smoke in the evening'), while Camille Soula (*Gloses sur Mallarmé*, p. 72) rearranges the word order of the stanza and makes 'du soir' a complement of the fourth verse ('Ne puisse surseoir à l'abandon du soir'). Finally, Charles Mauron (*Mallarmé l'obscur*, p. 189) has the originality of making 'fume' transitive; 'du soir' is the object, what 'is smoked.'
    I might have repeated the same partial yet oppressive review of exegetical disagreements concerning 'le doute du Jeu suprême' in the third sonnet of the triptych. I will content myself with noting the existence of these disagreements.
26   *Faux pas* (Paris: Gallimard, 1943), p. 191.
27   The last part of my sentence roughly translates this passage from a letter

quoted by Camille Mauclair in *Mallarmé chez lui* (Paris: Grasset, 1935),
p. 116. 'Je crois que toute phrase ou pensée, si elle a un rythme, doit
le modeler sur l'objet qu'elle vise et reproduire, jetée à nu, comme jaillie
en l'esprit, un peu de l'attitude de cet objet quant à tout. La littérature
fait ainsi la *preuve*; pas d'autre raison d'écrire sur du papier.' 'What
Mallarméan writing abolishes,' Yves Bonnefoy notes in a remarkable
passage on Mallarmés's 'realism,' 'is not our belief in the real flower,
but our notion of it in common practice.' ('La Poétique de Mallarmé,'
in Le Nuage rouge [Paris Mercure de France, 1977], p. 191).

28 in chaste crises, and in isolation, while the other gestation is going
on

That, precisely, is what modern man demands: to see himself, mediocre,
in a mirror...

29 set in motion by the collision of their inequality
30 ...this other paper wing is much more alive and succinct in its
unfolding, it hides the site in order to bring to our lips a silent painted
flower like the intact and inexistent word of a reverie approached by
the beating wing.
31 mutual reflections...like a virtual train of fire sweeping over precious
stones

similar themes...will balance, echoing one another from afar
32 use of thought laid bare, with its steps backward, prolongations, flights,
or its very design.

the mobility of the written work

Everything happens hypothetically, and seem foreshortened; a straight
narrative line is avoided.
33 *Mallarmé and the Art of Being Difficult*, pp. 116, 128, 132.
34 See *Mallarmé's 'Un Coup de dés'; An Exegesis* (New Haven: Yale
University Press, 1949). Richard interestingly speaks of the *Coup de dés*
as Mallarmé's 'clearest work, in any case his most explicit work'; it is
a 'temporal organism' supported by 'the focal solidity of a concept'
(*L'Univers imaginaire de Mallarmé*, pp. 563–4).
35 The sun which its supernatural / Halt exalts / Immediately descends
again / incandescent

I feel in my vertebrae / Darkness spreading out / All shivering / In
unison

And my head having surged up / A solitary look-out / In the
triumphant flights / Of this scythe

As a clean break / It suppresses or cuts short [settles] / The old
dissension / With the body

Rather than drunk with fasting / Stubbornly follow / In some haggard
leap / Its pure gaze

Up there where the eternal cold does not allow you – oh you glaciers – to surpass that gaze

But as for a baptism / My head illumined by the same / Principle which elected me / There bows a salutation [salute].

36 Robert de Montesquiou claimed to have learned from Mallarmé that St John would violate 'the mystery of [Hérodiade's] being' by looking at her; the saint would be put to death for this sacrilegious act. (Reported by Gardner Davies in *Les Noces d'Hérodiade*, p. 16.)

37 Noulet, for example, sees stanza 5 as expressing the saint's desire for his head to follow his look upwards (*L'Œuvre poétique de Stéphane Mallarmé*, p. 486). My own reading of stanza 5, and my translation, are in agreement with Jean-Pierre Richard's interpretation (in *L'Univers imaginaire de Mallarmé*, pp. 162–3 and 220), an interpretation also embraced by Cohn (in *Toward the Poems of Mallarmé*, p. 84).

38 Of a childhood feeling that amidst its reveries / Its cold precious stones finally begin to separate.

39 divided the disheveled tuft / Of kisses which the gods kept so well mingled.

40 In his remarks on Mallarmé's short essay 'Mimique,' Derrida interestingly speaks of Mallarmé's maintaining the differential structure of mimesis but without the Platonic or metaphysical notion of 'l'être d'un étant' which would be imitated. Mallarmé produces a wandering, unlocatable difference without any referents (see *La Dissémination*, p. 234).

41 But, enough! such a secret chose for confident / The vast and twin reed on which one plays under the blue sky: / Which, diverting to itself the cheek's agitation, / Dreams, in a long solo, that we were beguiling / The surrounding beauty by fictive / Confusions between itself and our credulous song, / And [dreams] of making – as high as love modulates – / Vanish from the every day dream of a back / Or of a pure side followed by my closed eyes, / A sonorous, illusory and monotonous line.

   Mauron encourages psychoanalysts to venerate this passage, in which the faun gives 'the poetic definition of all sublimation' (*Mallarmé l'Obscur*, p. 68).

42 slow prelude when the pipes start up...that flight of swans, no! of naïads.

43 To flee my lip on fire drinking, as a flash of lightning / Quivers! the secret terror of the flesh

INDEX